BAR BRICCO · BISTRO
· CAFÉ BICYO...E
TRO · THE COMMON ·
RIFT MOBILE EATERY/
SEN · DUCHESS BAKE
BILE KITCHEN · THE
AKAYA TOMO · JACEK
E · LANGANO SKIES ·
VILLAGE · MEAT · XIX
NORTH 53 · PADMANADI
· ROSTIZADO · SABOR ·
SOLSTICE SEASONAL
OWL · TRES CARNALES
H WHEEL · UCCELLINO
AIKA INDIAN BISTRO

Signature
Recipes
FROM THE
City's Best
▪ Chefs ▪

Edmonton
Cooks

TINA FAIZ & LEANNE BROWN

Figure 1
Vancouver / Berkeley

Cataloguing data available from Library and Archives Canada
ISBN 978-1-927958-52-0 (hbk.)

Design and art direction by Natalie Olsen
Photography by Dong Kim

Editing by Linda Pruessen
Copy editing and indexing by Iva Cheung

Printed and bound in China by C&C Offset Printing Co., Ltd.
Distributed in the U.S. by Publishers Group West

Figure 1 Publishing Inc.
Vancouver BC Canada
www.figure1pub.com

Dinner

details to come.

PHIL &
SEBASTIAN
COFFEE
ROASTERS

BOWS
ARROWS

To the beautiful city we call home
—LB & TF

DAILY
ROAST

>Pork<
Shoulder

w/chimichurri
& pickled red
onion

Contents

"What's your favourite restaurant in Edmonton?" This is the question we hear most often as food writers. And invariably, our answer is, "It depends." That's because, depending on the time of day, our mood, or even the weather, there are dozens of excellent eateries to satisfy our cravings — be it for slow-roasted Greek lamb, savoury green onion cake, delightful Key lime tart, or a plate of flawless ragu bolognese on a cold winter's night. (You'll find recipes for all of these dishes in this book, by the way!)

Food, of course, is more than just sustenance. It's a part of our identity. It's how we comfort ourselves. It's how we show love. Its symbolism defines cultures, but, most important, it bridges cultures. Breaking bread together is perhaps the most ancient and powerful form of bonding, and, in many ways, today's chefs are our modern-day cultural brokers — and creators.

Our beloved river city has experienced an impressive food renaissance in the last decade. The stalwart crew of restaurateurs who quietly delighted us for years are now joined by a new brigade of passionate farmers, butchers, bakers, and chefs who obsess over flavour, technique, and terroir. Many of them are featured in this book not only because they make spectacularly delicious food and warm us with hospitality but also because they care about where that food comes from, how it was raised, and how it impacts our community. Collectively, their gastronomic artistry makes a significant contribution to our city's vibrant culture; they make Edmonton a better place to live. With this book, we celebrate them and their craft.

In the pages that follow, you'll encounter chefs and recipes hailing from all parts of the globe. But the restaurants have

something in common: they are small and fiercely independent. Many are husband-and-wife owned, with buzzy rooms and killer cocktails.

In their open kitchens, tattooed chefs dish out creative plates with raw talent on full display. They take the best of our native land, with its beauty and bounty, and add their own cultural nods to make something uniquely Edmonton.

Edmonton Cooks is a triumphant collection of more than 70 chef-tested recipes from the city's best, hailing from Ethiopia to China, Philippines to Portugal, India to Italy — with dishes that range from comfort food to haute cuisine.

We're grateful to all the chefs who've opened their little black books and spilled the secrets to their signature dishes. Some recipes will push your culinary skills, but, with detailed instructions and invaluable

tips along the way, you'll feel as though the chefs are cooking alongside you in the kitchen.

Most chefs will tell you they're not in the food business — they're in the business of making people happy. They love creating an atmosphere, feeding people, and seeing the joy it brings. In turn, we hope their recipes inspire you to dine in tonight as if you were dining out, and share that joy with your loved ones. And on days you're too tired to cook, use this book as a guide for where to eat in the city — because there's plenty to chew on.

What's our favourite restaurant in Edmonton? Well, we wrote a book about it.

The Recipes

ACME
Meat Market

COREY MEYER
▪ *butcher* ▪

In Edmonton, there's an unwritten rule among chefs and discerning carnivores: if you need a good piece of meat—for a dinner party, a barbecue, or just a cozy night in front of the TV— ACME is the place to go. A Strathcona-area gem since 1921, ACME Meat Market is an old-school butcher shop, complete with wooden chopping blocks and butchers in white aprons. These days, however, it also has a decidedly modern-day mission: to source and sell hormone-free, antibiotic-free, grass-fed meat and free-run poultry—and preserve the nearly lost tradition of carving whole animals humanely raised near the city.

Butcher Corey Meyer and his wife, Amanda, serve as guides for those wanting to know where the meat on their plates comes from, how it was raised, and what it's eaten — all of which affects its taste and leanness. Corey learned at the apron strings of his father, a German-trained butcher, and graduated from the Northern Alberta Institute of Technology's meat-cutting program. (If there's any doubt about this third-generation butcher's dedication to his craft, check out the tattoo on his right forearm: it's a pig anatomy diagram, an image lifted from his father's old butchery textbook.)

Just as Corey followed in *his* father's footsteps, second- and third-generation Edmontonians have followed in theirs, shopping at ACME for its friendly service, custom cuts, and fresh sausages made in-store. Visitors can also pick up local grains, wild salmon, artisanal cheeses, jams, and mustards.

"I see myself playing an important role helping people who are trying to create dishes from scratch," says Corey. "I love it when a customer comes into the store and wants to recreate a dish that they had at a restaurant."

So, what are you waiting for? Grab your ingredients, and let's get cooking.

1 lb boneless short ribs
1 cup soy sauce
1–2 Tbsp grated fresh ginger
2 cloves garlic, minced
Juice of 1 lemon
Freshly ground black pepper

SERVES 4-6 *as appetizers*

Boneless Short Rib Skewers

CUT SHORT RIBS into ¼-inch slices and weave them onto 15 to 20 bamboo skewers. In a small bowl, combine soy sauce, ginger, and garlic. Place the skewers into a container large enough to hold them. Pour soy sauce mixture over the skewers. Drizzle with lemon juice and sprinkle with a pinch of pepper. Cover the container with plastic wrap and marinate overnight in the fridge. When ready to cook, grill skewers on high heat, about 90 seconds per side, and flip them only once. They'll cook quite quickly because they're thin, so watch that they don't over cook. Serve immediately.

Corey's Tips for Choosing the Perfect Steak

Begin by asking yourself how you want to prepare your steak. Grilling or marinating? For grilling, you want something tender, aged, and — if you're afraid of overcooking it — with a little fat. Have your butcher cut it between ¾ to 1½ inches for the grill. For marinating you will want something tougher, and you should talk to your butcher about options. Bonus: these steaks are usually less expensive.

At ACME we have 100% Pasture Raised Beef and/or Natural Beef that is finished on grain. You have to be comfortable with how the beef is raised, and with what it's eaten. Both will affect the final taste and the leanness of the meat.

Rib-eye steaks are the easiest for beginners to grill. They have a lot of fat marbling and are nearly impossible to overcook. They end up juicy and tender even if you leave them on the heat a little too long.

For less fat, choose striploin; the fat is external and can be trimmed after you finish grilling. Like the rib-eye, they stay juicy and tender when grilling and are good for novice steak cooks.

The most important thing you can do is get to know your butcher. They can tell you all about your steak: when it was cut, how much age it has, where it's from, and how to cook it. We can help you through the whole process and on your way to enjoying the best steak of your life. Lots of salt and pepper, some high heat, and you're away!

Best for **MARINATING**
Flank Steak
Skirt Steak
Flat Iron

Best for **GRILLING**
Rib-eye
Rib Steak (bone-in)
Striploin (bone-in or boneless)
T-Bone
Fillet Mignon
Top Sirloin

Clockwise from top right: rib-eye, top sirloin, flank steak, beef tenderloin, bone-in rib steak, T-bone, and striploin (centre).

Bar Bricco

DANIEL COSTA
owner

MICAH JOFFE
chef

The follow-up act to chef-owner Daniel Costa's Corso 32 (page 60), Bar Bricco is where Edmonton's fashionable nocturnal crowd hangs, listening to vinyl over a glass of wine and small, tasty bites. Daniel (pictured above) modelled his loud, sultry 28-seater after Italy's *spuntini* ("snack") bars — neighbourhood watering holes where you wind up after work or wind down your night. A ghoulish Vanguard Works mural echoes the bar's edgy atmosphere.

You can break the rules here and pick your wine first, then find nibbles to match. The 15-odd plates on offer run from total simplicity

(rare cured meats, aged cheeses, and freshly baked breads) to refined compositions (handmade pastas and crostini) that come in ideal portions for grazing and sipping.

As with Corso 32, you dine in a crowded fashion. Squeeze in at the woodtop for a fine Barolo and a plate of Eggs Moliterno *Cacio e Pepe*, creamy truffled eggs on crostini that are out of this world. On a blustery night, a glass of Amarone will warm you up, especially alongside a savoury lentil salad and unctuous cotechino sausage cut with a drizzle of saba, a tangy-sweet grape juice syrup. You can do a prosciutto tasting (yes, there is more than one kind), sliced à-la-minute for maximum freshness. Or try the playful Fonduta Agnolotti Dal Plin—delicate ricotta-stuffed pasta you gleefully dip in sage butter and roll in a snowy pile of Parmigiano Reggiano—and marvel at how chef Micah Joffe (pictured top right, with Daniel) rolls, fills, pinches, and cuts each one by hand.

No reservations needed at this hot spot, so pop in tonight.

¼ **cup** pine nuts

½ **cup** fresh lemon juice

1 **¼ cups** extra-virgin olive oil

1 **tsp** kosher salt

½ **cup** fresh or thawed frozen peas

6 **medium** very fresh zucchini

6 **handfuls** fresh pea shoots

Leaves of 4 sprigs fresh mint

Pecorino Romano, to taste, for finishing

Freshly ground black pepper

SERVES 4-6

Zucchini Carpaccio
with Pea Shoots, Mint, Roasted Pine Nuts, and Pecorino

PREHEAT THE OVEN to 350°F. Spread pine nuts on a baking sheet and roast for 5 to 10 minutes or until golden. Shake the tray every few minutes to ensure even browning.

MAKE VINAIGRETTE In a medium bowl, combine lemon juice, olive oil, and salt, and whisk until emulsified. Set aside.

If using freshly shelled peas, blanch peas in a pot of salted boiling water for 30 seconds. Then shock peas by quickly immersing them in a bowl of ice water. This helps keep their bright green colour and texture. Drain and reserve for the salad.

Using a vegetable peeler, peel the zucchini into long, ribbony strands on all sides down to the seeds; discard the core. Place strands in a bowl. Toss zucchini with a pinch of salt and enough lemon vinaigrette to just coat the strands. Season to taste. Pile the strands on chilled plates.

In another bowl, combine peas, pea shoots, and pine nuts. Roughly tear mint leaves and add to the bowl. Season with a pinch of salt and enough lemon vinaigrette to just coat the salad; taste and adjust seasoning. Scatter pea shoot salad evenly over zucchini. Using a fine grater, grate a small amount of Pecorino Romano over each salad. Finish with a fresh grinding of black pepper and serve immediately.

Tip: When zesting the lemon, use only the outer yellow layer. If you zest too deep to the white pith, the vinaigrette will become bitter.

LENTILS

½ **cup** beluga lentils

3 Tbsp extra-virgin olive oil

1 large carrot, diced

1 rib celery, diced

1 small yellow onion, diced

2 Tbsp red wine vinegar

Salt and freshly ground black pepper

Leaves of 3 sprigs flat-leaf parsley

SERVES **4** *as appetizers* **2** *as dinner*

Fried Cotechino
with Lentils, Carrot Salad, and Saba

Cotechino is a traditional Italian sausage made in many parts of northern Italy but most famously in Modena. **Cotechino** *comes from the word* **cotica** *(rind), because the sausage is made of pork shoulder and rind. Cotechino is traditionally eaten on New Year's Eve with lentils and is meant to bring you luck. Daniel likes to cut the fatty sausage with a drizzle of saba or* **vincotto** *("cooked wine," in Italian). Both are sweet-sour syrups made by reducing grape must or juice and can be found at most Italian markets.*

LENTILS Rinse lentils in a strainer to remove any debris. Put lentils in a small pot and add enough water to cover them by an inch. Bring to a boil then turn down to a simmer and continue to cook until lentils are just tender, about 20 minutes. Strain lentils, place them in a medium bowl, and set aside. You can make lentils a day in advance and store in the fridge, but bring them to room temperature before serving.

Heat olive oil in a large pan on high. Add carrots, celery, and onions. Cook until just about tender, about 5 minutes. Add cooked vegetables to lentils. To the bowl, immediately add vinegar and salt and pepper to taste. Stir in parsley. Allow to cool.

CARROT SALAD

1 large carrot, peeled
¼ small red onion, thinly sliced
Leaves of 2 sprigs flat-leaf parsley
Juice of ½ lemon
½ Tbsp extra-virgin olive oil
Kosher salt

ASSEMBLY

1 cotechino sausage (1 lb)
4–6 tsp saba or vincotto
Freshly ground black pepper

CARROT SALAD Just before serving, use a vegetable peeler to peel carrot into long strands, and place them in a bowl with onions, parsley, lemon juice, olive oil, and a pinch of salt. Toss to combine and adjust seasoning if needed.

TO ASSEMBLE Cut cotechino into 8 pieces, each about ¾ inches thick. Heat a large non-stick frying pan on medium. Place cotechino pieces in pan and fry until golden, about 3 minutes. Flip and continue cooking for another 3 minutes or until golden.

Place a scoop of lentil salad in the middle of each of 4 plates. Top with 2 pieces of cotechino. Place a small stack of carrot salad on top of the cotechino and drizzle with a little saba and a few cracks of black pepper. Serve immediately.

Bistro Praha

MILAN & SHARKA SVAJGR

ALENA BACOVKSY

DANIEL SCHULTZ
· *owners* ·

TY KOUCH
· *chef* ·

Menus that change daily may be in vogue, but Bistro Praha is sticking with tradition. "It's probably the only place on earth that has a menu that's stayed the same for 34 years," jokes co-owner Milan Svajgr. That's the staying power of Bistro Praha's artsy ambiance and authentic Eastern European fare. The Bistro's thin and crispy Wiener Schnitzel, famed Fried Breaded Cheese, and knock-out steak tartare have made it an institution in Edmonton's food scene, and a cozy purlieu to the city's theatre, literary, and symphony sets.

After a fire in the historic Kelly Ramsey block forced the Bistro to close, four long-time staff — Czech-born brother-and-sister duo Milan (above left) and Sharka Svajgr (not pictured) and their partners Alena Bacovsky (opposite, with chef Ty Kouch) and Daniel Schultz — reopened it a few blocks from the original location. "The menu is the same, the staff is the same, and it's the exact same furniture and the same 75 seats," Milan explains. Even the menu booklets were brought over, and the iconic Swiss Alps mural remains.

"The mural was the only thing damaged from the fire, and the day after we ordered a new one, a lady out of nowhere called us and said she had bought the exact same mural 33 years ago, and that we could come and pick it up," says Milan, still surprised at his luck.

Count yourself lucky, too. The Bistro's food is here to stay. Sometimes, it seems, change is overrated.

8 veal cutlets (5 oz each)
(or beef, pork, or chicken)
Salt and freshly ground black pepper
2 cups all-purpose flour

4 eggs, lightly beaten
2 cups bread crumbs
Lard or clarified butter, for frying
8 lemon wedges, for garnish

SERVES **4**

Wiener Schnitzel

PLACE ONE of the veal slices on a cutting board and cover with plastic wrap. Pound the meat with a mallet or a rolling pin until it is about ⅛ inch thick, being careful not to tear the meat. Repeat with the other cutlets.

With a sharp knife, make a few short cuts into the outer areas of the cutlets to prevent them from rolling up during the cooking process. Lightly season with salt and pepper on both sides.

On the counter, set up 3 shallow dishes. Fill one with flour, one with eggs, and the third with bread crumbs.

Coat both sides of each cutlet with a thin layer of flour. Pull each cutlet through the eggs, then coat with bread crumbs before placing on a cutting board. Using your hands, gently press down on the bread crumbs (this causes the coating to "fluff up" during frying), then shake off any excess.

Heat lard (which is traditional) or clarified butter in a large frying pan on medium. (There should be enough lard or butter so that the cutlet "swims" in it). To test if it is hot enough, drop a tiny sprinkle of bread crumbs into the pan. If they sizzle and brown quickly, it's ready. Once lard or butter is hot, place cutlets in the pan. Cook until they are golden brown on one side, then flip and cook until golden brown on the other. You can flip cutlets more than once if needed. When done correctly, the coating is crisp and brown but doesn't stick to the veal.

Before serving, rest schnitzel on a paper towel to let the oil drain. Serve with a wedge of lemon and a side of cold potato salad for a traditional meal.

1 goose (11–12 lbs)
2 **Tbsp** salt
3 **bulbs** garlic, minced, divided
3 large onions, chopped
5 **cups** cold water

2 **Tbsp** caraway seeds
⅔ **cup** port
1 **tsp** marjoram
Freshly ground black pepper

SERVES **6**

Roasted Goose

If you can't find a goose, substituting duck is just fine. Since ducks tend to be smaller than your average geese, be sure to shorten the cooking time so that you don't overcook the smaller bird.

PREHEAT the oven to 350°F.

Wash bird with cold water, pat dry with a paper towel, and remove excess fat, extra skin, neck, and giblets. Using a small, sharp knife or skewer, prick the skin of the whole goose, but avoid cutting the flesh. Rub with salt and about ½ cup of the minced garlic.

Line the bottom of a large roasting pan with chopped onions. Place the goose on top, breast up. Add cold water and sprinkle the whole pan and goose with caraway seeds. Cover with aluminum foil, making sure the sides are crimped tight to prevent steam from escaping as the bird cooks. Roast for 1½ hours.

Remove the roasting pan from the oven. Using a baster, remove the accumulated fat, reserving about 1 Tbsp for later use. Turn the goose over and roast, covered, for another hour.

Remove roasting pan from the oven and reserve pan juices for use later. Transfer the goose to a fresh pan, breast-side up, and roast uncovered for 15 to 20 minutes, until crispy and golden brown. Remove goose from the oven and allow it to rest while preparing gravy.

To make gravy, add reserved goose fat to a sauté pan on medium heat. Add remaining garlic and sauté for about 2 minutes. Add port and bring to a simmer. Cook until wine is reduced by half, 4 to 6 minutes. While the port simmers, strain the reserved pan juices. Once port is reduced, add strained juice and cook until mixture thickens slightly. Stir in marjoram and black pepper to taste.

Serve goose and gravy with sauerkraut and dumplings or red cabbage and parsley potatoes for a hearty, filling meal.

The Bothy

JADE PATTON
▪ *chef* ▪

CHRIS HUGHES
▪ *manager* ▪

DOUG TOWNSHEND
▪ *owner* ▪

Named after modest Scottish shelters for weary travellers, The Bothy is a smooth blend of whisky lounge, gastropub, and wine bar in the least likely of places—a strip mall along Edmonton's busiest thoroughfare.

The place has all you'd expect to find in a whisky bar—dark wood, leather chairs, a certain dim glow—but all eyes are on the sparkly wall of notable wines and, with over 175 varieties, the city's largest selection of whisky. It's certainly a draw for aficionados out "dusty hunting"—on the quest for old and rare spirits—but novices needn't be intimidated. The friendly and knowledgeable staff banish

any whiff of pretension. They'll happily explain the difference between whisky from the bluffs and glens of the Scottish Highlands (peaty and full-bodied) and those that hail from Speyside (sweet and elegant). Whisky, like wine, expresses the terroir and micro-climate of where it's made.

In case the thought crossed your mind, rest assured that the food here isn't just fortification for drinking. Chef Jade Patton's menu has a bit of something for everyone. There are small plates and DIY charcuterie boards, comforting chicken pies with flaky pastry (chock full of leeks, cream, and

white wine), and hearty steak sandwiches on chimichurri-buttered sourdough. And you don't have to wait until Robbie Burns Night to indulge in haggis, Scotland's national dish. Made with sheep's liver, oats, and spices, and cooked in a sheep's stomach, it's a spicy mince served with mashed tatties (potatoes), neeps (turnips), and a wee dram of whisky. *Slàinte mhath!*

3–4 cloves garlic, unpeeled

1 serrano chili, stem discarded

1 cup cilantro leaves

1 cup flat-leaf parsley leaves

¼ cup extra-virgin olive oil

2 Tbsp water

½ tsp salt

1 cup unsalted butter, room temperature

MAKES **4** *sandwiches*

The Bothy Steak Sandwich

This open-faced sandwich has several components, all of which can be prepared ahead of time. The Bothy makes its own mayonnaise (recipe below), but if you are pressed for time, a good-quality store-bought mayo will do the trick. Both the chimichurri butter and mayonnaise recipes will make more than you need for these sandwiches, but they're so delicious you'll be happy to have them around. You can freeze the butter and take it out to use in other sandwiches or melt onto roasted vegetables, baked potatoes, rice, or grilled fish. And the mayonnaise can be used just about anywhere.

CHIMICHURRI BUTTER Set a dry skillet on medium heat. Lay unpeeled garlic cloves and serrano chili in the pan. Roast, turning frequently, until soft and blotchy brown in spots, about 10 minutes for the chili and 15 minutes for the garlic. Cool, then slip skins off garlic.

Roughly chop garlic and chili and place in a food processor along with cilantro, parsley, olive oil, water, and salt. Process until smooth, but don't worry if it's not perfect; a few chunks are fine. Scoop into a bowl and taste. Add more salt if desired. Stir butter into the chimichurri until smooth.

Use immediately or scoop into a resealable plastic bag and store in the fridge or freezer for later use. It will keep well for 3 months in the freezer.

BOTHY MAYONNAISE

1 egg
1 Tbsp Dijon mustard
1 anchovy fillet, finely chopped
4 tsp white wine vinegar
(or fresh lemon juice)
Kosher salt
1 ⅓ cups vegetable or canola oil

BOTHY STEAK SAUCE

½ cup Bothy mayonnaise
3 Tbsp ponzu sauce
1 ½ Tbsp tahini
Salt and freshly ground black pepper

STEAK SANDWICH

2 medium onions
1 cup mushrooms of your choice
2 Tbsp butter, divided
4 Heritage Angus Beef rib-eye steaks
(6 oz each)
Salt and freshly ground black pepper
4 thick slices sourdough bread
4 Tbsp chimichurri butter
8 Tbsp Bothy steak sauce

BOTHY MAYONNAISE Add egg, mustard, anchovy, vinegar or lemon juice, and a pinch of salt to a food processor. Grind into a paste. With the food processor on, slowly pour oil in through the top spout and blend until incorporated. Taste and adjust salt and vinegar or lemon juice as needed. Pour into a lidded glass jar and store in the fridge for 3 to 4 days at most.

BOTHY STEAK SAUCE In a bowl, whisk all ingredients together. Adjust seasoning to taste.

STEAK SANDWICH Slice onions and mushrooms chunkier or more finely, according to your taste.

In a pan on medium heat, melt 1 Tbsp of the butter. Do the same in a second pan. Add onions to one pan and mushrooms to the other. Bring the heat down to low and slowly caramelize onions and mushrooms, checking occasionally and stirring. Add a little water to the pan if the vegetables are sticking. The mushrooms will take about 20 minutes to caramelize; the onions may take as long as 40 minutes. Combine vegetables and set aside.

Heat a griddle or frying pan on high. Sprinkle steaks generously with salt and pepper on both sides. Once the pan is hot, add steaks, either one at a time or together, depending on the size of the pan. Cook for 2 to 3 minutes on each side for medium rare, or to preferred doneness. Remove from the heat and allow steaks to rest for 2 minutes.

Meanwhile, butter one side of the sourdough bread slices with chimichurri butter and place under broiler. Toast until golden or darker brown, according to taste.

TO ASSEMBLE Place a chimichurri toast on each of 4 plates. Top with rib-eye, onions, and mushrooms. Drizzle with steak sauce (or serve it on the side for dipping) and top with another slice of toast. Serve with your favourite salad.

OVEN-DRIED TOMATOES
3–4 ripe tomatoes
¼ cup extra-virgin olive oil
¼ cup balsamic vinegar
2 cloves garlic, minced
Fresh rosemary and oregano, to taste

VANILLA CLAM BUTTER
¼ cup unsalted butter, room temperature
¼ tsp vanilla bean paste
1 tsp clam bouillon
2 tsp fresh lemon juice

GENTLE LEMON GARLIC AIOLI
4 cloves garlic
⅔ cup milk, divided
1 cup mayonnaise
2 Tbsp fresh lemon juice
Salt and freshly ground black pepper
Ingredients continued overleaf

SERVES **4**

Crispy Salmon
with Potato Salad di Roma

You'll need some advance prep work for this dish — all the better to enjoy your company (and not be stuck in the kitchen). The oven-dried tomatoes are effortless but do need to be left overnight. Make a double or triple batch and store them in the fridge to add instant flavour to sandwiches and pastas. Rehydrated sun-dried tomatoes can be easily substituted here if you're short on time.

OVEN-DRIED TOMATOES Preheat the oven to 125°F and line a baking sheet with parchment paper. (A barely warm oven creates a dehydrator-like environment.) If your oven's lowest setting is 170°F, simply reduce the cooking time to 8 to 10 hours.

Cut each tomato into 6 segments and place in a large bowl. Add olive oil, vinegar, and garlic. Mix well and marinate for 5 minutes (no longer or the balsamic flavour will be too strong).

Place tomatoes, rosemary, and oregano on the baking sheet. Place tomatoes in the oven to dry for 10 to 12 hours, until meaty and concentrated in flavour. If making ahead, store in the fridge until ready to use.

VANILLA CLAM BUTTER In a bowl, mix all ingredients until smooth and uniform. Spread a large piece of plastic wrap on the counter and place butter mixture along the centre in a log shape. Roll butter log in plastic and refrigerate for at least 30 minutes.

GENTLE LEMON GARLIC AIOLI In a small saucepan on medium heat, cover your garlic with a third of the milk. Bring milk to a boil. Immediately remove the saucepan from the heat and strain garlic. Repeat this poaching process twice more with the rest of the milk.

Thinly slice the poached garlic and place it in a small bowl. Add mayonnaise, lemon juice, and a pinch of salt and pepper, and stir to combine. Adjust seasoning to taste.

Recipe continued overleaf

WARM POTATO SALAD DI ROMA

1 lb baby potatoes
Salt
3 Tbsp fresh lemon juice
(zest lemon first and use for salmon)
¼ cup extra-virgin olive oil

¼ cup water
Freshly ground black pepper
2 oz mascarpone
1 Tbsp capers
Oven-dried tomatoes

SALMON

¼ cup finely chopped flat-leaf parsley
¼ cup finely chopped fresh dill
Zest of 1 lemon
1 Chinook salmon fillet (about 1 ½ lbs), skin on
2 Tbsp vegetable oil
4 Tbsp vanilla clam butter
Salt and freshly ground black pepper

WARM POTATO SALAD DI ROMA In a medium pot, cover potatoes with water and add a pinch of salt. Cover and bring to a boil on high heat. Turn heat to medium and let simmer until tender, 15 to 20 minutes. Drain and let potatoes cool.

Meanwhile, make the potato salad dressing. In a small bowl or Mason jar, combine lemon juice, olive oil, water, and generous pinch of salt and pepper. Whisk or shake to combine and set aside.

Heat a pot on medium-low and add 2 to 3 Tbsp of dressing, mascarpone cheese, capers, and oven-dried tomatoes.

Break up the prepared baby potatoes in your hands or on the countertop. Add to the pot to warm. Season to taste with salt and pepper, and keep warm until ready to serve.

SALMON In a small bowl, mix parsley, dill, and lemon zest.

Place salmon fillet on a cutting board, skin-side up. You'll need to make diagonal slits, spaced half an inch apart, along the entire length of the filet to create pockets for the herb stuffing. Starting at one end of the salmon and using a sharp knife, cut through the skin and stop when you are halfway into the flesh. Repeat until you reach the other end. Stuff the herb and lemon mixture into each crevice, and sprinkle salmon with salt and pepper. You can cut the salmon into 4 equal portions now, before frying, or after, depending on the size of your frying pan.

Heat oil in a large frying pan on medium-high. When oil is shimmering in the pan and begins to smoke, place salmon in the pan skin-side down. Cook for about 6 minutes. Flip salmon, add vanilla clam butter to top of fillet, and continue cooking for another 2 minutes. (Salmon at The Bothy is cooked to medium, but you can adjust the cooking time according to your taste.) Remove from the heat. Allow salmon to rest for about 1 minute before slicing into 4 portions (if it wasn't sliced before).

TO ASSEMBLE Place a quarter of the potato salad in the centre of each of 4 plates. Spoon aioli onto the side and place salmon on top of potato salad. Garnish with a little parsley and drizzle plate with additional potato salad dressing. Serve with sautéed fresh vegetables, if desired.

Café Bicyclette

JOHN LAU
▪ *chef* ▪

FRANCK BOUILHOL
▪ *pastry chef* ▪

In an ideal world, we'd all have a neighbour-hood restaurant we love: a cozy bistro around the corner, a place that's both a second home and a refuge from the everyday, a place where the menu reads like a beloved novel and the staff are like neighbours.

The French Quarter has such a spot, and though I don't live nearby, I pop in enough to claim Café Bicyclette as my own. As an outsider —and one of the non-French-speaking variety— I love watching this vintage-meets-Paris– decorated café bring the community together over croissants and café au lait. Evocative *bal-musette* accordion plays while friends

greet one another with not one but two kisses on the cheek.

French language flows as easily here as the luscious Rhone wines, which only adds to the atmosphere. Breakfast is served all day, with omelettes, croque monsieurs, and delectable poutine. On a Sunday, one of baker Franck Bouilhol's irresistible pastries, with a coffee or pot of Cally's Tea, is a well-earned reward after shopping at the adjoining farmers' market for organic breads and farm-fresh eggs.

Toward the weekend, and as day turns to night, the café transforms into a romantic French restaurant. Steaming plates of

Moules et Frites or Ratatouille with Goat Cheese Polenta are delivered to lucky diners, who finish off their meals with a delightful crème brûlée or tarte au citron. Gaggles of laughter spill outdoors to the year-round patio, where a roaring fire, warm blankets, and hot drinks take the frosty edge off of winter. And in this northerly metropolis, that's an approach we can all embrace. — **TF**

CRUST

½ cup unsalted butter, room temperature
¼ cup granulated sugar
Salt
1 vanilla bean
1 egg
1 ⅔ cups all-purpose flour

LEMON CURD

1 ½ sheets gelatin (gold)
¾ cup cold water, for gelatin
½ cup fresh lemon juice
Zest of 1 lemon
⅔ cup granulated sugar, divided
2 eggs
½ cup unsalted butter, diced (½-inch cubes)

MERINGUE

¼ cup water
2 cups granulated sugar
3 egg whites, room temperature

SERVES **8-10**

Lemon Tart

This delightful lemon tart is sunshine on a plate. (It calls for lemon zest, so find unsprayed lemons if you can.) It's perfect on its own, says Franck Bouilhol of FanFan Pastries Limited, who bakes for the cafe, but if you want to — ahem — tart it up even more, dot it with teardrop-shaped meringue, bring out your fancy tea cups, and relish its beauty, because it will be too pretty to eat. Well, almost.

CRUST Using a stand mixer fitted with a paddle attachment or an electric mixer, cream together butter, sugar, and a pinch of salt.

Using a small knife with a sharp point, split vanilla bean in half and scrape out seeds. Add seeds and egg and mix into the butter mixture until light and fluffy.

Using a wooden spoon, stir flour into the mixture until just incorporated. Do not overmix or the dough will become tough and difficult to work with.

Turn the dough onto a clean surface and, using your hands, press and form into a rough circle about 9 inches in diameter. Wrap in plastic and chill until firm, about 30 minutes.

Once the dough is cool, remove it from the fridge and allow it to sit at room temperature for 5 minutes, or else it can crack and split. Preheat the oven to 350°F.

With your fingers, press dough evenly into the bottom and up the sides of a 9-inch tart pan with a removable bottom, and prick in several places with a fork (this will prevent bubbles and uneven baking). Bake for 15 to 20 minutes, until the crust is a light golden brown. Remove it from the oven and allow to cool completely.

Recipe continued overleaf

LEMON CURD Lay gelatin sheets flat in a bowl, add cold water, and allow to sit for 3 to 5 minutes (this ensures gelatin will dissolve evenly in lemon curd).

In a saucepan on medium heat, bring lemon juice, zest, and ⅓ cup of the sugar to a boil.

While lemon juice mixture heats, whisk eggs with the remaining ⅓ cup sugar in a large stainless steel bowl until sugar dissolves. Once the lemon mixture comes to a boil, pour it very slowly into the egg and sugar mixture, whisking continuously.

Return the mixture to the saucepan and cook over low heat, whisking continuously until mixture thickens enough to coat the back of a spoon. Remove the saucepan from the heat when the first bubble appears (this should take 6 to 8 minutes). Remove gelatin sheets from the water, squeezing out excess moisture. Off the heat, add gelatin to lemon curd and whisk to incorporate.

Pour lemon curd into a bowl and refrigerate until it comes to 104°F, or is semi-hot to the touch. Remove from fridge and slowly add the butter. Allow butter to melt and then, using a hand mixer, purée until smooth, 2 to 4 minutes. If butter doesn't melt too easily, don't worry — the mixer will work it in. This process of "mounting" will lighten the curd up and make it a little fluffy.

Tips: Don't use Knox gelatin here instead of the sheets — your lemon curd will be too stiff. When zesting the lemon, use only the outer yellow layer. If you zest too deep to the white pith, the curd will become bitter.

TO ASSEMBLE Pour lemon curd into baked tart shell and refrigerate until completely cool and the curd is set, at least 1 hour. Slice and serve — or add meringue before serving.

Tip: If you're concerned about salmonella or have a weakened immune system, consider using pasteurized eggs for the meringue.

MERINGUE In a small pot on low heat fitted with a candy thermometer, combine water and sugar and stir until sugar is dissolved. Increase heat to medium-high and allow syrup to come to a boil. Cook syrup until its temperature reaches 244°F.

Meanwhile, in a stand mixer fitted with the whisk attachment (or using an electric mixer in a large bowl), whisk egg whites until stiff peaks form. When syrup is ready, and with mixer on low, pour syrup slowly into the egg whites along the edge of bowl. Gradually increase speed to high and mix until meringue is voluminous and you get glossy, stiff peaks. Take extra care the syrup doesn't hit the whisk as you pour it, or it may splash hot syrup and burn you.

Fill a piping bag with the meringue. Pipe teardrop-shaped dollops of meringue on the finished tart, as little or as many as you like. Using a culinary torch, lightly caramelize the meringue until golden brown, and serve. Store any leftovers in the fridge for up to 5 days.

GOAT CHEESE POLENTA

2 Tbsp extra-virgin olive oil
1 Tbsp minced garlic
¾ cup minced yellow onions
2 cups milk
2 cups vegetable broth
1 cup cornmeal
1 cup corn kernels
½ cup goat cheese

RATATOUILLE

3 Tbsp extra-virgin olive oil, divided
2 Tbsp minced garlic
1 cup minced yellow onions
1 cup white wine
2 cups diced zucchini (1-inch cubes)
2 cups sliced mushrooms
2 cups diced red peppers (1-inch cubes)
1 cup diced eggplant (1-inch cubes)
1 cup diced red onions (1-inch cubes)
3 cups tomato paste

4 cups vegetable stock
1 tsp chopped fresh thyme
1 tsp chopped fresh oregano
1 tsp salt
½ tsp freshly ground black pepper

ASSEMBLY

Canola oil, for frying
Microgreens, parsley, or fresh thyme
leaves, for garnish

SERVES **6-8**

Ratatouille
with Goat Cheese Polenta

GOAT CHEESE POLENTA Butter or spray a 9 × 9-inch pan with non-stick spray. Line with parchment paper.

Heat olive oil in a large pot on low. Add garlic and onions and sauté until translucent but not brown, about 10 minutes. Add milk and vegetable broth and turn up the heat until liquid begins to simmer.

Once liquid is simmering, slowly pour in cornmeal, whisking continuously. Return heat to low and whisk until all of the liquid has been absorbed, about 20 minutes. Remove from the heat and stir in corn and goat cheese.

Pour polenta mixture into the prepared pan. Smooth as evenly as possible with a spatula. Cover with plastic wrap and allow to cool completely in the fridge for up to a day.

RATATOUILLE Heat 2 Tbsp of the olive oil in a saucepan on low. Add garlic and onions and sauté until translucent but not brown, about 10 minutes. Add white wine and simmer until reduced by half, about 10 minutes.

Meanwhile, heat the remaining 1 Tbsp olive oil in another large saucepan on medium-low.

Add zucchini, mushrooms, red peppers, eggplant, and onions, and sauté until golden brown and soft, about 20 minutes.

Once the wine has reduced in the first pot, stir in tomato paste, vegetable stock, thyme, oregano, salt, and pepper. Simmer for 15 minutes.

Add tomato sauce to the vegetable mixture and cook for another 5 minutes.

TO ASSEMBLE Cut polenta into 6 or 8 portions, depending on how many you are serving.

In a cast-iron frying pan, add canola oil until there is about an inch in the pan. Heat on medium to 340°F — or, to test if it's hot enough if you don't have a thermometer, carefully dip the handle of a clean wooden spoon into the oil, and when bubbles form around the handle, it's ready. Fry polenta pieces until golden brown on one side, then flip and do the same on the other. It should take about 2 minutes per side. (A deep fryer can also be used for this step.)

Place each serving of polenta on a plate and top with ratatouille. Finish with microgreens or a sprinkle of chopped parsley or thyme, if desired.

Canteen

MIKE NGUYEN

▪ chef ▪

When self-taught chef Frank Olson and his wife, Andrea, opened Canteen in their own Westmount neighbourhood, area residents wanted to keep it to themselves. But word about the new hot spot on the city's "it" culinary street spread fast, and the place remains packed every weekend.

Seventeen years and three kids after opening their stellar Red Ox Inn (page 160), Frank and Andrea have created a new kind of hip-yet-elevated restaurant, delivering Ox's fine-dining sensibilities in a more casual, trendy setting, with a long concrete bar, oversized pendant lights, and wood tables.

At dinnertime, the 50-seat eatery is a buzzy, hopping room. A diverse crowd—from natty thirtysomethings to their retiring parents—visit over wine and nibble on Corn Fritters with Smoky Maple Syrup, and Milk-braised Turkey Leg with Golden Spätzle that tastes like Thanksgiving on a plate.

Unlike the evening-only Ox, Canteen is open all day, and executive chef Mike Nguyen's menu nods to our local bounty, with Irvings Farm ham, local eggs, and vegetables from Reclaim Urban Farm. For lunch, expect creative salads and small plates. A mid-afternoon between-errands pit stop might include bacon-wrapped,

chorizo-stuffed dates. Order a glass of wine, too. We won't judge.

Mike's creativity is also on display on Canteen's wildly popular brunch menu, with savoury-sweet fixings that hit the spot: chicken with Belgian waffles, Dutch baby pancakes with rhubarb compote and back bacon, or poached eggs on cheddar biscuits with sausage and gravy. With a midday meal like this, who needs dinner?

TURKEY

2 medium onions, chopped
4 ribs celery, chopped
2 medium carrots, chopped
2 turkey legs (about 1 lb each)
4 cups whole milk
8 cups chicken stock

1 Tbsp whole black
peppercorns
5 sprigs fresh thyme
3 sprigs fresh rosemary
½ bunch parsley, chopped
2 bay leaves

SPÄTZLE

1 ½ cups all-purpose flour
¼ cup cornmeal
5 tsp kosher salt, divided
2 eggs
⅓ cup grainy mustard

⅓ cup + 1 Tbsp milk
⅓ cup + 1 Tbsp water
1 tsp saffron threads, ground
a bit with your fingers
Ingredients continued overleaf

SERVES **4**

Milk-braised Turkey Leg
with Golden Spätzle and Crispy Chicken Skin

TURKEY Preheat the oven to 425°F.

Place onions, celery, and carrots in a roasting pan large enough to hold the turkey legs. Nestle turkey legs on vegetables, pour milk and chicken stock overtop, and toss in peppercorns, thyme, rosemary, parsley, and bay leaves.

Roast, covered, for 2 hours, or until meat is tender and falls off the bone. Remove the roasting pan from the oven, and reserve all of the braising liquid inside pan.

When turkey is cool enough to touch but still warm, shred meat by hand, removing hard tendons and bones.

Strain braising liquid and pour just enough of it over the shredded turkey to cover the meat. Reserve the remaining braising liquid, refrigerating until needed.

SPÄTZLE In a large bowl, whisk together flour, cornmeal, and 1 tsp of the salt.

In another bowl, whisk together eggs and mustard. Add milk, water, and saffron, and whisk to combine.

Make a well in the centre of the flour mixture and pour in the wet ingredients. Whisk slowly to incorporate. Continue whisking until smooth, then allow the batter to rest for 1 hour in the fridge (no need to cover).

When ready to cook spätzle, prepare a large bowl of ice water and set it on the counter. Fill a large pot with water, add remaining 4 tsp salt, and bring to a boil on high heat. Place a spätzle maker or a colander with large holes over the pot. Pour about a third of the spätzle batter into the colander and use a rubber spatula to force the batter through the holes. Remove the colander. Once the spätzle start to float, cook for another minute or until set and puffy.

Recipe continued overleaf

4 pieces chicken skin
Salt and freshly ground
black pepper
¼ cup butter
2 Tbsp canola oil
3 cups diced ham
3 cups peas
½ lb arugula

When spätzle are done, remove from boiling water with a slotted spoon and drop into the ice water to stop the cooking. Repeat this process until you have used all of the spätzle batter. Drain the cooked spätzle well and refrigerate for up to 3 days until ready to serve.

TO ASSEMBLE Preheat the oven to 350°F.

Line a baking sheet with parchment and stretch chicken skins flat. Cover with another layer of parchment and then another baking sheet (this will keep the skins flat as they crisp). Bake for 20 minutes.

Remove the top pan and season skins with a pinch of salt and pepper. Remove skins from the pan if they are golden brown and most of the fat has rendered off; if not, bake uncovered for another 5 minutes. Remove from the oven, drain off any excess fat, and allow to cool.

In a large frying pan on medium heat, melt butter. Add shredded turkey and 1 cup of the leftover braising liquid. Cook until liquid has thickened and reduced to coat turkey. Adjust seasoning to taste.

To prepare spätzle, heat oil in a large non-stick frying pan on high until oil starts to smoke slightly around the edges. Remove the pan from the heat to add the spätzle (careful: oil may splatter). Shake the pan gently so that spätzle do not stick. Return the pan to high heat and cook, stirring occasionally, until spätzle are golden and crispy. Add ham, peas, and arugula, and stir for about 3 minutes until heated through.

Spoon spätzle onto 4 plates. Top with turkey mixture and finish off by crumbling chicken skins over the top of each plate.

SEMIFREDDO

2 ⅓ cups + ½ cup whipping
(35%) cream, divided
2 cups granulated sugar, divided
6 egg yolks
½ cup water
2 Tbsp unsalted butter
1 tsp sea salt
Ingredients continued overleaf

SERVES **4**

Hey Hey Cake
with Rum Syrup, Smashed Sponge Toffee, and Salted Caramel Semifreddo

*Hey Hey Cake is Mike's take on a **baba au rhum**—the rich, yeasted cake soaked in booze so beloved in Europe that almost every country has its own version. Semifreddo ("half-cold" in Italian) is a velvety frozen treat that marries the richness of ice cream with the airiness of mousse. Best of all, you don't need an ice cream machine to make it. If you're pressed for time, you can easily substitute store-bought ice cream in this recipe.*

SEMIFREDDO Combine 2 ⅓ cups of the cream and ¾ cup of the sugar in a large bowl. Using an electric mixer, whip until soft peaks form. Set aside.

In another bowl, beat egg yolks and ¼ cup of the sugar with a whisk (or wash the mixer and use it here) until doubled in volume and pale yellow. Set aside while you prepare the caramel.

In a saucepan on medium heat, cook the remaining 1 cup sugar and water until sugar turns a dark amber colour (keep an eye on it, because it will turn colour quickly). Remove from the heat, add the remaining ½ cup cream, and whisk to incorporate (it will foam up a bit as the cold cream meets the hot sugar). Add butter and whisk until you have a smooth, golden caramel. Add salt and mix through. Set aside to cool for about 10 minutes.

When caramel has cooled down a bit but is still warm, slowly drizzle one half into the cream mixture and the other half into the egg yolk mixture. Using a stand mixer (or electric mixer) whip each again until soft ribbons form. Using a spatula, fold the two mixtures together. Pour into an airtight container and freeze for at least 8 hours, until solid.

Recipe continued overleaf

RUM SYRUP
1 cup water
1 cup granulated sugar
⅓ cup dark rum
Zest of 1 lemon
Zest of 1 orange

CAKE
1 cup all-purpose flour
1 Tbsp granulated sugar, plus more for sprinkling cupcake moulds
1 tsp salt
1 tsp instant yeast
2 eggs, room temperature
3 Tbsp unsalted butter, melted
2 tsp warm water
Butter, for greasing cupcake moulds
Rum syrup

SPONGE TOFFEE
Butter, for greasing
½ cup + 1 Tbsp granulated sugar
⅔ cup corn syrup
2 tsp baking soda, sifted

BUCKTHORN PURÉE
2 cups frozen buckthorn berries (or frozen apricot or apricot purée)
½ cup granulated sugar

ASSEMBLY
2 cups walnut pieces, lightly toasted

RUM SYRUP In a saucepan on medium heat, combine all ingredients and bring to a boil. Once sugar is dissolved, remove syrup from the heat, strain out zest, and cool until needed.

CAKE Preheat the oven to 400°F. In a bowl, stir together flour, sugar, salt, and yeast. Add eggs one at a time, mixing in between with a wooden spoon. Add butter and water. Knead dough for 5 to 7 minutes, until smooth and elastic. Divide dough into 6 equal pieces.

Butter 6 cupcake moulds and sprinkle with sugar. Place a piece of dough in each mould. Coat a piece of plastic wrap with non-stick spray and place — oiled side down — over the moulds to seal.

Allow the cakes to rise in a warm place on the counter for about 1 hour until doubled in size. Remove the plastic wrap. Place moulds in the oven and bake for 12 minutes, or until a skewer inserted into the centre of the cake comes out clean. Remove the cakes from the cups. While cakes are still hot, soak with cooled rum syrup. Set aside until ready to serve.

SPONGE TOFFEE Grease a 7 × 12 ½-inch loaf pan with butter.

In a medium saucepan on high heat, bring sugar and corn syrup to a boil and cook until mixture reaches 305°F on a candy thermometer. Immediately sprinkle baking soda overtop and whisk quickly to distribute evenly (the mixture will bubble violently).

Pour the mixture into the loaf pan and allow it to cool undisturbed at room temperature until completely hardened, about 10 minutes. Remove it from the pan and smash it into large chunks.

BUCKTHORN PURÉE Soak frozen berries in just enough warm water to cover berries, and allow them to thaw. Drain three-quarters of the water. Using an immersion blender, gently purée without breaking up seeds. Strain the seeds and discard them. Place the remaining liquid in a small saucepan, along with sugar. On medium heat, cook until the mixture is thick and syrupy, 5 to 10 minutes.

TO ASSEMBLE Preheat the oven to 200°F.

Heat cakes until just warm in centre, about 2 minutes. Plate with a scoop or slice of semifreddo on the side and pieces of sponge toffee sprinkled overtop. Top with toasted walnuts and finish with a drizzle of buckthorn purée.

Cibo Bistro

ROSARIO CAPUTO
• *chef & owner* •

One of the joys of dining at husband-and-wife-owned Cibo Bistro — where they cure their own meats and hand-roll pasta made from scratch — is the vicarious (and customs-free!) tour of Italy through its outstanding seasonal menu.

Within minutes of perusing the all-Italian wine list, you're instantly beamed onto the rolling hills of Tuscany, with its old and wise Sangiovese vines planted with military precision as far as the eye can see. Before you know it, that antipasto of arancini you ordered is a vision of Arborio rice paddies near Milan.

NAIT-trained chef Rosario Caputo hand rolls, breads, and deep-fries creamy mushroom risotto with a hint of sage for a potato-chip-crisp outside and an oozy Fontina cheesiness inside. (He's Italian; it's in his blood.) Carne Cruda offers a quick jaunt to the mountainous Piedmont region of northwestern Italy. Made simply with olive oil, lemon, fresh chives, and mushrooms (as Piedmontese do, rather than egg yolk), this raw, diced beef tenderloin is a marvel of flavour and texture. And the hearty Orecchiette with Rabbit Sausage takes you south to Puglia, Italy's most flat and fertile growing region. The ears of durum wheat pasta are like little hands cupping savoury bits of sausage and puddles of garlicky white wine tomato sauce.

Whether you're simply looking for an excellent meal with excellent service or sorely in need of a trip down Italy's glorious country roads (even imaginary ones), Cibo Bistro is just the ticket.

3 oz beef tenderloin or eye of round, finely chopped
5 Tbsp extra-virgin olive oil, divided
1 Tbsp chopped fresh chives
1 Tbsp fresh lemon juice

Salt and freshly ground black pepper
2 oz beech mushrooms, chopped (or other fresh, seasonal mushrooms)
1 oz Pecorino Romano, grated
2–4 crostini

SERVES 2-4 *as an appetizer*

Carne Cruda Piemontese

IN A SMALL BOWL, combine beef, 3 Tbsp of the olive oil, chives, and lemon juice. Add salt and pepper generously to taste. Mix until just combined. Set cruda aside until ready to serve.

Heat 1 Tbsp of the olive oil in a sauté pan on medium heat. Add mushrooms and cook for 5 to 6 minutes, until light brown. Set aside to cool. You should have about 1 oz of cooked mushrooms.

Pile cruda in the centre of a serving plate and top with mushrooms. Sprinkle Pecorino Romano overtop and drizzle with remaining 1 Tbsp olive oil. Finish with a dusting of pepper. Serve with crostini.

Tip: Beech mushrooms can be hard to find. If you don't have them in your area, substitute with what's seasonal and available. Cremini, porcini, and chanterelles will all work beautifully.

RABBIT SAUSAGE

½ lb rabbit meat

3 oz pork fatback

2 cloves garlic, roasted

Leaves of 1 sprig fresh thyme

1 Tbsp salt

½ Tbsp freshly ground black pepper

Zest of 1 lemon

ORECCHIETTE

2 Tbsp extra-virgin olive oil

½ cup diced carrot

½ red onion, diced

½ cup diced celery

4 cloves garlic, sliced

¼ cup chicken stock

¼ cup dry white wine

1 can (28 oz) whole San Marzano tomatoes

Salt and freshly ground black pepper

20 oz orecchiette, fresh or dry

⅓ cup finely grated Parmigiano Reggiano

SERVES **4**

Orecchiette
with Rabbit Sausage

Making your own sausage meat is as simple as fixing your morning coffee. All the ingredients go into a machine, and out comes a perfectly seasoned mixture ready to use right away. You can easily substitute Italian pork sausage meat in this recipe, but then you won't get to say, "I made the sausage myself!"

RABBIT SAUSAGE In a large bowl, combine all ingredients. Put mixture through a meat grinder or food mill. Stir to ensure ingredients are well incorporated, but do not overmix. (It will ruin the texture.)

ORECCHIETTE Heat olive oil in a medium saucepan on medium. Add carrots, onions, celery, and garlic and sauté until onions are translucent, about 5 minutes. Do not let the vegetables become brown. Reduce heat to medium-low, add rabbit sausage, and cook for about 30 minutes, stirring occasionally.

Add chicken stock and white wine and simmer until liquid is reduced by half, 5 to 7 minutes. Crush the canned tomatoes roughly with your hands and add them to the pot. Simmer for about 45 minutes. Taste and season with salt and pepper. Keep sauce on a low simmer until pasta is ready.

TO SERVE When ready to serve, bring a large pot of water seasoned heavily with salt to a boil. If using fresh orecchiette, boil for 3 minutes. If using dry orecchiette, boil for 7 to 10 minutes or according to package instructions.

Add cooked pasta to the sauce and stir to coat. Remove the pot from the heat. Ladle orecchiette and sauce into pasta bowls. Sprinkle each dish with Parmigiano Reggiano and pepper to serve.

The Common

JESSE MORRISON-GAUTHIER

▪ *chef* ▪

We could call The Common a gastropub, but the label seems inadequate for the many roles this eclectic legislature-grounds hangout plays throughout the day.

It all starts with a lively noon hour. The tufted-leather banquettes fill quickly with government workers and politicos lunching on chef Jesse Morrison-Gauthier's spicy chicken and bacon waffles and tasty salads. His menu is a godsend in this part of town, where good food can be hard to come by.

The scene changes when happy hour rolls around, and the black-and-white interior (and small patio in the summer) subtly morphs into

a cocktail bar. Young unbuttoned business types unwind and trade political gossip over a craft brew and truffled popcorn or winey mussels and fries. If it's been a particularly long or bad day, a two-person, pitcher-sized cocktail may be in order. The Sangrita is a spirit-lifting concoction of Grand Marnier, raspberry peach juice, fresh berries, and Prosecco. And not sharing is perfectly acceptable.

As the sun sets, the bar animates and the volume gets louder. Friends dine on Seared Scallops with Rhubarb Agrodolce (a sweet-sour Italian reduction), irreverently dusted with crushed popcorn. Subsequent dishes—

like Spaghetti Squash with Brown Butter, Pine Nuts, Feta and, Brussels Leaves (so tasty you won't miss the meat)—confirm Jesse's ingenuity. A NAIT and Packrat Louie alum, he is as thoughtful as his cooking is varied.

When night falls and the DJ calls the dancers to the floor, one thing becomes perfectly clear: The Common is anything but.

4 slices prosciutto
¼ cup butter, room temperature
½ cup grated Gruyère
½ cup grated Parmigiano Reggiano
¼ cup finely chopped chives
12 eggs
½ cup whipping (35%) cream

Salt and freshly ground pepper
2 Tbsp bread crumbs
1 small wheel (5.2 oz) Boursin cheese
(shallot and chive flavour)
1 cup chopped garden herbs
(e.g., tarragon, parsley, chervil, basil)

SERVES **4**

Oeufs en Cocotte
with Prosciutto

PREHEAT the oven to 395°F.

Line a baking sheet with parchment paper and arrange prosciutto slices on the sheet so that they aren't touching. Lay another sheet of parchment over the slices and then place another baking sheet on top. (This will weigh the prosciutto down so that it stays flat as it crisps up.)

Bake for 12 minutes or until prosciutto is mahogany coloured and crisp. Remove prosciutto from tray and place onto a paper towel to drain excess grease. Set aside.

Reduce oven to 350°F.

Bring a medium pot of water to a simmer (or heat water in a kettle).

Evenly coat each of 4 large ramekins with a quarter of the butter. Sprinkle about 1 Tbsp each of Gruyère and Parmigiano Reggiano and 1 ½ tsp of chives into each ramekin. Crack 3 eggs into each ramekin and then add 2 Tbsp cream to each. Sprinkle with a pinch of salt and pepper and stir the mixture slightly, but do not break yolks. Top each ramekin with remaining Gruyère, Parmigiano Reggiano, and chives.

Place ramekins in a high-sided baking dish and fill dish with enough hot water (from the pot or kettle) to come halfway up the sides of the ramekins (a *bain marie*).

Gently place the baking dish on the middle rack of the oven and bake for 18 minutes or until egg yolks are cooked to your preference.

Place a crisp piece of prosciutto on top of each ramekin. Top with bread crumbs, crumbled Boursin, and herbs. Finish with freshly ground black pepper.

POPCORN DUST
2 Tbsp canola oil
½ cup popcorn kernels
¼ cup melted butter
Salt and freshly ground
black pepper

AGRODOLCE
2 ½ cups extra-virgin olive oil
¾ cup hazelnuts
½ small red onion, finely diced
1 shallot, finely diced
4 ribs celery, finely diced
¼ cup sultana raisins
½ cup drained capers

½ cup red wine vinegar
½ cup cauliflower florets
1 stalk fresh rhubarb,
finely diced (or ½ cup frozen)
¼ cup honey
(clover honey is best)
Salt and freshly ground
black pepper

SCALLOPS
1 Tbsp canola oil
8 large scallops, U/10 size
Kosher salt and freshly
ground black pepper

ASSEMBLY
Crackers of your choice
(Jesse prefers a flat-
bread-style cracker)

SERVES 4

Seared Scallops
with Rhubarb Agrodolce and Dusted Popcorn

POPCORN DUST Heat oil for 1 minute in a large pot on medium-high. Add popcorn kernels and cover with a lid. Gently shake the pot, moving constantly until kernels begin to pop aggressively, then reduce heat to medium. Once kernels stop popping, remove the pot from the heat.

Pour popcorn into a large bowl and season with melted butter, salt, and pepper to taste. Once popcorn is cool, pour it into a resealable plastic bag and smash with a rolling pin or potato masher until it is dusty and fine.

AGRODOLCE Heat olive oil in a large sauté pan on medium. Toast hazelnuts in the oil until golden brown. Remove hazelnuts from oil with a slotted spoon and set aside on a paper towel to drain.

To the same pan add onions, shallots, celery, raisins, and capers. Sauté for about 5 minutes on medium heat. Add vinegar and cook for about another 5 minutes.

Remove pan from the heat and pour contents into a large bowl. Add cauliflower, rhubarb, and honey and stir to combine. Taste and season with salt and pepper.

SCALLOPS Heat oil in a non-stick pan on high. Meanwhile, sprinkle scallops with salt and pepper on both sides. When oil is shimmering and begins to smoke, place scallops in the pan and cook on one side until deep mahogany brown, 2 to 3 minutes (cook on one side only). Remove scallops from the heat and set them on a paper towel to dry.

TO ASSEMBLE Spoon equal amounts of agrodolce into 4 serving bowls. Place 2 seared scallops on top and sprinkle with kosher salt and popcorn dust. Serve with crackers.

Tip: If you want extra points for presentation, wrap scallop in a leek sleeve before searing.

Corso 32

DANIEL COSTA
owner

MATT GUERIN
chef

When Corso 32 opened in late 2010 to enormous hype—and six-week waits for a table—I figured I'd inevitably be disappointed. What could live up to that? So I waited.

A year and a half went by before I discovered how chef Daniel Costa (pictured right) magically transforms simple but quality ingredients into dishes worthy of the countless accolades, the celebrity guests—and all that hype.

Chef Ben Chalmers (left) took the lead in the kitchen after the opening of Bar Bricco (page 14), but Matt Guerin (centre) is currently the chef of this 34-seat modern Italian hot spot. Together, these thirtysomething chefs

express the Platonic ideal of Italian classics like traditional Ragu Bolognese on handmade tagliatelle—pasta so good it'll haunt your dreams. Inside the cool-yet-cozy room—with its requisite brick wall, communal wood table, and understated signage—the pair consistently executes flawless modern renditions of Italian favourites with professional service. Their obsessively fine-tuned menu is short, seasonal, and stacked with dishes so beloved—creamy whipped ricotta made with Fairwinds Farm goat milk; spoon-tender deep-fried short rib with thin sheets of shaved pear and peppery arugula; polenta with pork shoulder braised in what

seems like liquid gold—there'd be a revolt if any were taken off the menu.

But what I love most is Corso 32's unadvertised create-your-own-adventure eating. Feel like splitting a pasta course? No problem. Want half-pours of different wines to pair with each course? Sure thing. Can't choose what to order? The five- and eight-course tasting menus (with optional wine pairings) turn your indecisiveness into a virtue. And all this, capped off with a decadent chocolate torta. I just wish I hadn't waited so long to find out.
—**TF**

1 lb ricotta, drained in a
fine-mesh strainer overnight
1 egg
⅔ cup Parmigiano Reggiano,
freshly and finely grated
½ Tbsp kosher salt

Pinch of nutmeg, freshly grated
2 Tbsp all-purpose flour
5 egg yolks
4 ½ lb semolina
¼ cup unsalted butter
1 Tbsp fresh lemon juice

5 large leaves of Swiss chard,
stems removed and leaves cut
into large pieces
Parmigiano Reggiano, grated,
for finishing
Freshly ground black pepper

SERVES 5

Egg Yolk Gnudo
with Swiss Chard and Parmigiano

*Gnudo means naked in Italian, and that's
exactly what it is — the ricotta filling of
a traditional raviolo, denuded of its pasta
robe. If you want to elicit gasps of awe
from your guests, serve these delicious
morsels and watch their joy when the
luscious egg yolk hidden inside spills out.*

PLACE ricotta, whole egg, Parmigiano
Reggiano, salt, and nutmeg in a large bowl.
Mix with your hands until well combined.
Sprinkle flour over the mixture and mix in
until just combined. Allow mixture to chill
in fridge for 1 hour.

Meanwhile, place 1 lb of the semolina in a
shallow, flat-bottomed casserole-style dish.
You should have a nice bed of semolina and
enough room to fit 5 gnudi dumplings — a
9 × 12-inch dish or larger should be fine.

Take ricotta mixture out of the fridge, and,
working quickly, form it into five 2 ½ oz balls
and five 1 ½ oz balls. These will form the tops
and bottoms of your rounded ricotta dumplings; you will tuck an egg yolk in between.

To make one dumpling, begin by making
a small indent in the 2 ½ oz ball, just large
enough to fit an egg yolk. One way to do
this is by gently placing the dumpling
on a clean surface lined with parchment
paper and pushing the curved back of a
melon baller (or small ice cream scoop or
tablespoon measuring spoon) gently into
the ricotta ball, taking care not to push too
far. Crack a fresh egg and separate the yolk
from the white. Very gently place yolk in the
indent you just made. To cover the egg yolk,
gently flatten a 1 ½ oz ricotta ball in your
hand until it matches the size of the 2 ½ oz
piece. Place the smaller piece on top of the
egg yolk. Dip your hands in cold water and
very gently seal the seam. Delicately roll it
into a ball by rotating the dumpling in your
hands. Immediately place the ball in the
semolina-lined dish, and roll it around so
that it's lightly coated.

Recipe continued overleaf

Repeat this process until all five dumplings are made. Gently pour remaining 3 ½ lbs semolina over the gnudi to completely cover. Place dish in the fridge and allow to cure for at least 36 hours, and ideally for 48 hours. You can leave the dish uncovered if you like, or cover with plastic wrap. During this time, the semolina will drain moisture away from the dumplings and form a thin "semolina skin" that will hold it together during cooking.

When ready to serve, bring two medium pots of salted water to a boil. While water is boiling, gently melt butter in a third, small pot. Add a splash of water, lemon juice, and a pinch of salt. Whisk to emulsify and keep warm.

In the first pot, cook Swiss chard in boiling water for 30 seconds or until just tender. Drain and keep warm.

Gently remove gnudi from the semolina and, using a large slotted spoon, very gently place them in the second pot of boiling water. Turn the heat down slightly to ensure the water is simmering and not rapidly boiling. Cook gnudi for 7 minutes. Meanwhile, place Swiss chard in the centre of 5 warm plates. Using a spider or slotted spoon, very gently remove each gnudo and place it on top of the Swiss chard. Spoon a little of the emulsified butter sauce over each gnudo, top with a generous sprinkling of freshly grated Parmigiano Reggiano and black pepper, and serve immediately.

4 **Tbsp** extra-virgin olive oil
½ **cup** + **2 Tbsp** butter, divided,
plus more if needed
2 ½ **cups** ground pork
2 ½ **cups** ground beef
(fatty, preferably beef chuck shoulder)

¾ **cup** pancetta, very finely chopped
1 ½ **Tbsp** kosher salt, divided
1 ½ **cups** finely chopped carrots
1 ½ **cups** finely chopped celery
1 ½ **cups** finely chopped onions
10 **cracks** black pepper (about 1 tsp)
¾ **cup** tomato paste

2 **cups** whole milk
1 **cup** water
1 **small** Parmigiano Reggiano rind
1 **cup** dry white wine
750 **g** dry tagliatelle
¼ **cup** grated Parmigiano Reggiano,
plus more for finishing

SERVES **6-8**

Ragu Bolognese

HEAT OLIVE OIL and ½ cup of the butter in a 10- or 12-inch heavy-bottomed pot on medium-high. Add ground pork, beef, pancetta, and 1 Tbsp of the salt. Cook for 10 to 15 minutes or until the meat is dark golden. Stir frequently with a wooden spoon to break up the meat and to prevent burning. Add carrots, celery, onions, pepper, and the remaining ½ Tbsp salt, and cook for another 15 minutes, stirring frequently; add a little more butter if needed.

Lower heat to medium and add tomato paste. Mix it into the meat and vegetables and cook for 1 minute, stirring constantly. Add milk, water, and cheese rind. Lower heat and simmer with lid ajar for 40 minutes.

Add white wine and continue to cook ragu for another 30 minutes. Remove from the heat and allow ragu to rest for 30 minutes. Adjust seasoning with salt and pepper.

To cook pasta, bring a large pot of salted water to a boil. Cook tagliatelle until al dente. Drain pasta and reserve 1 cup of its cooking water.

While the tagliatelle is cooking, reheat ragu on high heat in a large enough pot or pan to comfortably hold all of the pasta. Add tagliatelle to the ragu, along with a couple of splashes of pasta cooking water and the remaining 2 Tbsp butter. Stir to combine. Ragu should just coat the pasta but not be dry. Add a little more pasta water if needed. Remove from the heat and gently stir in grated Parmigiano Reggiano. Serve immediately with a little more freshly grated Parmigiano on top.

Culina

BRAD LAZARENKO
▪ *owner* ▪

STEPHANIE ALCASABAS
▪ *chef at Muttart* ▪

STEVEN FURGIUELE
▪ *chef at Mill Creek* ▪

On a sleepy residential street in Mill Creek lined with grand elm trees, Brad Lazarenko quietly revolutionized dining in Edmonton. When he opened Culina on the first day of spring in 2004, it stole our hearts and raised our expectations of what a neighbourhood restaurant ought to be — a casual place where locally sourced ingredients are prepared with creativity and infinite care.

From day one, the black-and-white decor, boho vibe, and slow-food ethos have been the core of Culina's staying power. Brad was buying directly from local farmers before it became trendy, and with that bounty he continues to dish out internationally inspired comfort food with bold flavours borrowed from France

to Turkey, Italy to India. The man can cook anything (and well), but he's as humble as his food is audacious: from steak with blue cheese and chocolate sauce to phyllo parcels filled with chana daal, goat cheese, and spicy, tangy-sweet tomato chutney — everything is worth the judgmental glares as you lick your plate.

These days, Brad is on a mission to bring local food to the masses. He's built a bustling café inside the iconic Muttart Conservatory, and transformed stodgy clubhouse fare at the city's public golf courses with his trio of Dogwood Cafes. "I'm continuing my love affair with the river valley," he says, serving Nordic brunches, locally roasted Iconoclast coffee, and local beer on tap.

Stephanie Alcasabas heads the kitchen at Muttart with a killer brunch, where a visit to the pyramid's lush gardens — followed by juicy Green Onion Cakes with Braised Pork and Kimchi — is a delicious refuge on a blizzardy winter's day.

Culina Mill Creek will close when its lease comes up this year. But its talented chef de cuisine, Steven Furgiuele, will continue to be part of the Culina family, supplying Culina (and other local restaurants) stellar charcuterie through Fuge Meats, a new venture Brad helped him launch. Spicy andouille sausages, local lamb salami, and peppery beef bresaola are all on the menu — and all lovingly made by hand in small batches, just like Steve's father used to do in Portugal. Thankfully, Culina's quiet revolution and creative menus live on.

1 **Tbsp** ghee or extra-virgin olive oil

1 **Tbsp** finely chopped onions

½ **Tbsp** minced garlic

½ **Tbsp** minced fresh ginger

¾ **cup** tomato paste

1 **Tbsp** Tandoori curry paste
(like Patak's brand)

½ **cup** water

1 bay leaf

1 **tsp** salt

½ **tsp** freshly ground black pepper

1 **cup** cooked chickpeas

1 **tsp** fresh lemon juice

1 **Tbsp** chopped cilantro

SERVES **8**

Goat Cheese and Chana Daal
Baked in Phyllo Pastry

This delicious and elegant vegetarian main is served with sautéed greens and Brad's famed tomato chutney, a recipe inspired by renowned Indian cookbook author Madhur Jaffrey. It delivers a punch of zingy, sweet-spicy flavours to the creamy, earthy bundles. You might have a bit more chana daal and chutney than you'll need, but don't worry — you'll find a use for them. At Culina, the chutney has made cameo appearances on frittatas, poached eggs, salmon, and chicken. It's equally tasty on a ricotta-topped crostini.

CHANA DAAL In a medium saucepan on medium heat, warm ghee or olive oil. Add onions, garlic, and ginger and sauté until they darken a bit, about 5 minutes.

Add the tomato and curry pastes and cook for about 10 minutes until the ghee begins to separate from the paste. Add water, bay leaf, salt, pepper, and chickpeas and cook until the mixture thickens, 10 to 15 minutes. Add lemon juice and cilantro and taste. Adjust seasoning with salt and pepper if needed.

Remove the pan from the heat, discard the bay leaf and, using an immersion blender, roughly purée the mixture (it should retain a bit of texture). Set aside. This can be made in advance and keeps well in the fridge for 3 to 4 days.

TOMATO CHUTNEY

½ **cup** minced garlic
½ small onion, chopped
3 Tbsp grated fresh ginger
2 Tbsp olive oil
1 can (28 oz) diced tomatoes
⅓ **cup** brown sugar, packed
1 Tbsp sambal oelek
(a southeast Asian garlic chili sauce;
use any garlicky hot sauce you like)

1 Tbsp Tandoori curry paste
1 Tbsp salt
1 Tbsp freshly ground black pepper
1 tsp ground cinnamon
1 tsp smoked paprika
1 tsp ground turmeric
1 tsp vanilla
½ **tsp** ground fennel seeds
½ **tsp** ground coriander seeds
½ **tsp** dried fenugreek leaves

PHYLLO PASTRY

1 lb goat cheese
16 sheets phyllo pastry
¼ **cup** ghee or extra-virgin olive oil

SAUTÉED GREENS

¼ **cup** extra-virgin olive oil
2 bunches rapini, broccolini, kale,
or asparagus (whatever is in season),
cut into bite-size pieces
Salt
Fresh lemon juice, to taste

TOMATO CHUTNEY In a food processor, grind garlic, onions, and ginger, or chop as finely as you possibly can with a knife.

Heat olive oil in a medium saucepan on medium. Add garlic, onions, and ginger mixture and sauté until lightly brown, about 10 minutes.

Add tomatoes, brown sugar, sambal oelek, curry paste, salt, pepper, cinnamon, paprika, turmeric, vanilla, fennel seeds, coriander seeds, and fenugreek. Stir to combine, and bring to a simmer on medium heat. Reduce heat to medium-low and simmer for 20 to 30 minutes until thickened slightly. Set aside. Stores well in an airtight container in the fridge for 3 to 4 days.

PHYLLO PASTRY Preheat the oven to 400°F and line a baking sheet with parchment paper.

Cut goat cheese into 8 pieces. Place one piece of goat cheese in the middle of 2 sheets of phyllo pastry and top with 3 Tbsp of chana daal. Wrap the phyllo around the goat cheese and daal to make a neatly packaged rectangle. Fold the sides onto the cheese, and fold it over a few times like a letter.

Place phyllo bundle on the parchment-lined baking sheet and brush with ghee or olive oil. Repeat with remaining phyllo, goat cheese, and daal, and bake parcels for 12 minutes or until golden.

While parcels are baking, heat chutney and prepare greens.

SAUTÉED GREENS Heat olive oil in a large sauté pan on medium. Once oil is hot (it should shimmer and flow around the pan easily), add greens to the pan with a pinch of salt. Sauté until greens are bright green and tender enough that a fork goes through them easily. Top with lemon juice and adjust seasoning with salt to taste.

TO ASSEMBLE Spoon about ½ cup warm chutney onto a plate and place one phyllo parcel on top. Layer greens overtop or on the side, squeeze a bit more lemon juice on top, and serve.

1 head napa cabbage

2 Tbsp salt

¼ cup soy sauce

½ cup chopped green onions

1 Tbsp minced fresh ginger

1 Tbsp minced garlic

2 Tbsp Korean chili paste (preferably gochujang)

2 tsp sesame oil

1 Tbsp rice vinegar

GREEN ONION CAKES

2 ½ cups all-purpose flour

1 cup warm water

8 tsp sesame oil

1 bunch green onions, finely chopped

2 tsp coarse kosher salt

½ cup canola oil

SERVES **8**

Green Onion Cakes
with Braised Pork and Kimchi

The kimchi recipe included here is a "quick" version, not the traditional fermented-for-weeks type. Even so, it takes two days to prepare, so give yourself time for this step; it's worth the wait.

KIMCHI Finely shred cabbage. Toss with salt, put in a colander set in a larger bowl to catch the drippings and refrigerate overnight.

The next day, rinse cabbage in cold water and squeeze out any excess water. This will help keep the cabbage crunchy.

Place cabbage in a large bowl. In another small bowl, whisk together soy sauce, green onions, ginger, garlic, chili paste, sesame oil, and vinegar and pour over cabbage. Mix with your hands, cover, and leave in the fridge overnight. The kimchi can be used the next day, but it will also keep for a couple of weeks in a jar in the fridge.

GREEN ONION CAKES In a large bowl, mix flour and water together until a soft dough forms. Knead dough for about 2 minutes, until smooth and elastic. Drip a few drops of vegetable oil over the ball of dough to coat and place it back in the bowl, cover with plastic wrap, and allow it to rest for 30 to 60 minutes in the fridge. The resting will make the dough more elastic and easier to roll out.

Cut the dough into 4 equal pieces. Lightly oil the back of a large metal baking sheet or a smooth stone countertop or pastry board. Roll out one piece of dough until it is a very large, thin rectangle, about 12 × 9 inches. If you have trouble with the dough sticking to the counter, you can use a bit of extra flour, but try not to add too much or the dough will get too dry and won't roll out as thin.

Drizzle 2 tsp of the sesame oil over the rolled-out dough. Use a pastry brush to make sure the dough is evenly coated. Sprinkle a quarter of the green onions over the dough and then sprinkle liberally with ½ tsp kosher salt. Remember that there is no salt in the dough, so this salt will be bringing out all of the flavour in the final cake.

2 cups water

1 Tbsp smoked paprika

1 Tbsp salt

½ cup soy sauce

1 cup chopped white onions

1 Tbsp ground cumin

1 Tbsp freshly ground black pepper

2 ¼ lb boneless pork shoulder

ASSEMBLY

4 Tbsp olive oil

4 cups mixed lettuce

2 tsp sesame seeds, toasted, for garnish

Roll the dough up tightly, like a carpet. Cut the long rolled-up piece in half and coil each half into a snail shape. Set aside to rest while you roll out the other pieces.

When all pieces are complete, it is time to assemble the cakes. Starting with the first piece of dough you made, roll the coil of dough to flatten it into a pancake shape, roughly 5 inches in diameter. This process creates the flaky layers of dough in the final cake. Repeat with remaining pieces.

Heat a 10-inch heavy frying pan or sauté pan on medium-high heat, and add a healthy glug of oil, about ¼ cup to start. When oil shimmers, lay a pancake of dough gently in the pan. It should sizzle but not burn. Cook for 2 minutes on one side, then flip and cook for another 2 minutes until golden brown. Transfer onto a paper towel to drain excess oil. Repeat with the remaining green onion cakes, adding more oil to the pan as needed. (You may not need the full ½ cup.)

Tip: You can buy excellent frozen green onion cakes at Lucky 97 if time is an issue. They are made here in Edmonton.

BRAISED PORK Preheat the oven to 325°F.

Fill a roasting pan with the water, paprika, salt, soy sauce, onions, cumin, and black pepper. Gently place the pork shoulder into the centre of the pan. Cover with aluminum foil and braise pork for 3 to 4 hours, or until the meat is tender when a fork is inserted.

Allow pork to cool at room temperature, then pull meat apart with forks and mix with the pan juices. Set aside.

TO ASSEMBLE In a medium sauté pan, heat olive oil on medium heat and add pork. Sauté about 5 minutes or until some bits of pork are crispy. Remove from the heat.

Warm green onion cakes in a pan or in a 200°F oven.

Place one green onion cake on each plate and top with a handful of mixed lettuce, about ½ cup crispy pork, and 3 Tbsp kimchi. Sprinkle with toasted sesame seeds and serve.

Drift Mobile Eatery / Dovetail Delicatessen

NEVIN & KARA FENSKE

▪ *owners* ▪

"We drifted around the globe," says Red Seal chef Nevin Fenske, explaining the inspiration behind his food truck's name. Along with his wife, Kara, Nevin travelled to five continents over five years, exploring street food cultures from Slovenia to Thailand. In 2011, they returned home and began combining all of those flavours in craft sandwiches served out of their restaurant on wheels.

Their bestseller, the pork belly, has created a new standard for what a sandwich should be: well travelled, locally sourced, and delicious. It's Drift's take on a Vietnamese bánh mì, made from moist slices of braised then seared local

pork belly tossed in hoisin glaze, topped with chili mayo, cilantro, pickled carrots, and daikon inside a light sourdough bun. Round it out with hand-cut fries spiced with cumin, fennel, and chilies — and don't forget Nevin's homemade ketchup, simmered for three hours and finished with cardamom and ginger. If those spices make you think of the Indian subcontinent, it's for good reason. Nevin's Pakistani-Polish heritage helps him mingle East and West flavours with ease.

No surprise, really, that Drift's success begat a successor. In 2015, Nevin and Kara opened Dovetail, a light-filled delicatessen and carvery where, every day, a fresh roast is carved and stuffed into fresh German buns. The cooler is stocked with homemade samosas, salads, pâté, dips, and savoury tarts, should the mood for an impromptu picnic strike. And home cooks take note: this is also where you can pick up a personal supply of Drift's spice mix and famed ketchup to recreate the full food truck experience at home.

PORK BELLY
8 ½ cups chicken
or pork stock
¼ pork belly
(or 2 lbs skinless belly)
Salt and freshly ground black pepper
Ingredients continued overleaf

Pork Belly Sandwich

You might wonder if all this work is worth it for a sandwich; the answer is always a resounding yes. Each component — the chili mayo, the pickled vegetables, the braised pork belly — can be made ahead of time and refrigerated, so that when the craving strikes (and it will, often) or you have a crowd to feed, you can simply heat and assemble it in your own kitchen and play food-truck at home.

PORK BELLY Preheat the oven to 300°F.

In a large stockpot on high, heat stock until boiling.

Liberally season pork belly on both sides with salt and pepper.

In a large frying pan on medium heat, sear both sides of pork belly until dark brown. Place belly in a roasting pan, fat-side down, and pour in the hot stock to cover three-quarters of the belly. Place in the oven and braise for 3 hours, turning once halfway through.

Remove pork belly from oven and allow to cool to room temperature. Place between two pans with a weight on top to compress it. This process will make the pork release more fat and allow for easier slicing. Pork belly can be refrigerated overnight.

Recipe continued overleaf

PICKLED DAIKON AND CARROTS

1 small daikon, cut into matchsticks
2 large carrots, cut into matchsticks
1 tsp salt
1 tsp + 3 Tbsp sugar, divided
1 cup white vinegar
1 cup warm water
1 tsp chili flakes

CHILI MAYO

1 Tbsp vegetable oil
¼ cup finely diced red onions
1 clove garlic, minced
2 Tbsp minced fresh ginger
1 tsp chili powder
¾ cup mayonnaise
1 tsp fish sauce
1 tsp lime juice
1 tsp brown sugar, packed
1 tsp sriracha

ASSEMBLY

2 Tbsp canola oil
5–10 Tbsp hoisin sauce
5–6 buns
Leaves of 1 small
bunch cilantro

PICKLED DAIKON AND CARROTS Place daikon and carrots in a bowl and sprinkle with salt and 1 tsp of the sugar. Massage to extract water and soften. Rinse thoroughly with tap water and drain. Place daikon and carrots in a non-reactive container with vinegar, warm water, chili flakes, and the remaining 3 Tbsp sugar. Allow to sit for at least 1 hour in the fridge; it will keep, refrigerated, for up to 2 weeks.

CHILI MAYO Heat oil in a skillet on medium, and sauté onions, garlic, and ginger until they begin to soften, about 3 minutes. Add chili powder and cook another minute. Remove from the heat and allow to cool.

In a bowl, mix mayonnaise, fish sauce, lime juice, brown sugar, and sriracha. Add onion mixture and stir to combine. This recipe makes about 1 cup. Leftovers will keep in the fridge for 3 to 4 weeks.

TO ASSEMBLE Cut pork belly into ¼-inch slices.

Heat oil in a sauté pan on medium-high and sear cooked pork belly slices until crispy, 1 to 2 minutes on each side. Place in a bowl and toss with hoisin sauce so that each slice is coated.

Warm buns. For each sandwich, spread 2 to 3 tsp chili mayo on one side of the bun. Layer on 4 to 5 slices of pork. Top with a handful of pickled daikon and carrots and 4 to 5 cilantro leaves.

6 yellow potatoes, peeled

2 Tbsp canola oil

1 medium yellow onion, minced

3 cloves garlic, minced

1 thumb fresh ginger, minced

1 Tbsp ground cumin

1 Tbsp ground coriander seeds

1 Tbsp kosher salt

2 tsp mustard seeds

½ tsp garam masala

½ tsp hot paprika

½ tsp ground turmeric

2 tsp malt vinegar

2 tsp white vinegar

1 cup green peas, blanched

½ cup water

1 package samosa wrappers (25 wrappers), thawed (like Serenna brand)

Canola oil, for frying

CORIANDER CHUTNEY

4 Tbsp sultana raisins

1 Tbsp minced fresh ginger

1 bird's-eye chili

2 tsp fresh lemon juice

1 tsp ground cumin

½ tsp salt

Sunflower oil (if needed)

2 bunches cilantro

MAKES **25** *samosas*

Potato and Pea Samosa
with Coriander Chutney

SAMOSAS In a large pot of salted water, boil potatoes until just cooked, so that a fork pushes easily all the way through the potato, 15 to 20 minutes. Allow to cool and dice into small, pea-sized pieces and place in a large bowl.

Heat oil in a large sauté pan on medium. Sauté onions, garlic, and ginger for about 7 minutes, or until soft. Remove from the heat and set aside.

In a small bowl, mix cumin, coriander, salt, mustard seeds, garam masala, paprika, turmeric, and vinegars until a paste forms. Add this paste to the onion mixture, and sauté for about 1 minute. Mix in peas and water (to deglaze the pan). Add the pea mixture to potatoes.

To assemble samosas, follow the instructions on the back of the samosa wrapper package. You can use a deep fryer to cook samosas, or deep-fry them in a pot. Heat oil to 350°F, and fry for 5 to 6 minutes or until golden and crispy.

CORIANDER CHUTNEY In a bowl, submerge sultanas in hot water until soft, about 3 minutes, then strain them and place them in a food processor. Add ginger, chili, lemon juice, cumin, and salt and blend until smooth. If needed, add sunflower oil to thin out the mixture slightly. Add cilantro in batches and process until smooth. This recipe makes 1 cup chutney. Leftovers will keep in the fridge for 1 to 2 weeks.

Duchess Bake Shop

GISELLE COURTEAU
· *owner* ·

If you've ever been to Duchess Bake Shop, you make it a top priority to go back again. And again, and again. Partly, it's to devour what you fell in love with on that first trip (my crush was the Paris Brest, a delicate ring-shaped pastry stuffed with ethereal praline mousseline and caramelized hazelnuts). But you also return to this enchanting place for its airy and elegant ambiance, its bustling vibe evocative of a Renoir social gathering, and, of course, to discover a new sweet temptation.

One of the first to move in to the now-hot 124 Street district, Duchess lured Edmontonians to a tiny escape to Paris, with its colourful

macarons, buttery brioche, and legendary tarts. The sweet, warm smell of vanilla and butter draws you like a hypnotic spell toward exquisite galettes, madeleines, and flaky croissants artfully displayed on antique silver trays. Resistance is futile, so order one of each. And don't you dare skip the Key Lime Tart—a hand-shaped graham crust filled with implausibly creamy, tangy goodness.

After dozens of awards and a bestselling cookbook, Duchess has justifiably become famous for its painstakingly scratch-made pastries, baked fresh daily. What started out as an operation with seating for ten in a narrow

café has grown to a brisk business that makes 10,000 macarons per week. And it's still growing.

With Jacob Pelletier's classic pastry training (and stages at famed Fat Duck and Sketch in London), Giselle Courteau's vision and determination, and Garner Beggs's affable personality and entrepreneurial drive, the trio of owners—a modern family of sorts—have built a beloved patisserie that's put Edmonton on the culinary map. And we're so grateful they did! —TF

1 ¼ **cups** graham cracker crumbs
3 Tbsp granulated sugar
½ cup unsalted butter, melted,
plus more for greasing
2 egg yolks

1 Tbsp firmly packed grated Key lime zest
(about 4 limes—or substitute regular limes)
1 ¼ cups sweetened condensed milk
½ cup fresh Key lime juice
(4–6 limes—or substitute regular limes)

MAKES **4** *tarts*

Key Lime Tart

These Key lime tarts are made using four 4-inch tart or pastry rings that are 1 to 1 ½ inches high. Alternatively, you can use an 8-inch pie plate.

PREHEAT your oven to 300°F. Line a baking sheet with parchment paper and arrange the tart rings or pie plate on it.

MAKE CRUST In a bowl, combine graham cracker crumbs, sugar, and butter. Stir until graham crumbs are moist and stick together slightly when clumped. If using tart rings, place about ½ cup of the crumb mixture into one of the rings. Using your fingers, gently press crumbs up the sides of the ring to cover.

Fill in the bottoms with the crumbs that remain. Repeat for the remaining rings.

If using a pie plate, lightly grease the plate with butter and press crumbs evenly along the bottom and sides using your fingers. Bake tart shells for 12 minutes, or pie crust for 14 minutes. Remove from the oven and set aside.

Increase oven to 325°F.

In a bowl, whisk together egg yolks, lime zest, and condensed milk until smooth. Slowly pour in lime juice and whisk again until smooth. Using an ice cream scoop or a large spoon, fill the baked tart shells or pie crust level with the top. Bake tarts for 10 minutes, or pie for 18 minutes. Allow to cool for 10 minutes before gently removing the tart rings. Refrigerate for at least 2 hours before serving, until fully chilled. (Tarts will keep in the fridge for up to 4 days.)

PIE DOUGH
2 cups all-purpose flour
½ cup unsalted butter, cold,
diced (½-inch cubes)
½ cup vegetable shortening, cold,
diced (½-inch cubes)
½ tsp salt
½ cup ice-cold water

MAKES **1** *pie*

Saskatoon Pie

Saskatoon berries are purple-skinned, gold-fleshed orbs akin to tangy blueberries. They are native to the Prairies, the North, and parts of the United States and grow wild in backyards, along walking trails, and in our beloved river valley. Duchess sources theirs from Farmer Wade Fossum of Berry Ridge Orchard, about 45 minutes northeast of Edmonton. For a variation on this pie, Giselle suggests you halve the recipe for saskatoon filling, spread a layer of fresh raspberries over the bottom of the pie shell, top with saskatoon filling and the crumble, and bake as instructed.

PIE DOUGH Place flour, butter, shortening, and salt into the bowl of a stand mixer fitted with a paddle attachment. Mix on low speed until the fats are in small chunks and the mixture looks a bit dry. This should take only 10 to 15 seconds. If you overmix, you'll have a difficult time incorporating all of the water in the next step.

Add ice water all at once and mix on medium speed until dough just comes together. Some small lumps of fat should remain in the dough.

Shape dough into a ball, wrap in plastic wrap, and refrigerate for at least 30 minutes, making sure dough is fully chilled before rolling out. At this point, the dough could be frozen if you plan to assemble the pie at a later time. Allow it to thaw completely before using it, but when you roll it out, be sure it's still cold.

To form the pie shell, lightly flour your work surface and place cold pie dough in the middle. Lightly flour the top of the dough and, using a

CRUMBLE TOPPING

½ cup old-fashioned rolled oats

⅓ cup all-purpose flour

⅓ cup brown sugar, packed

¼ tsp ground cinnamon

¼ cup unsalted butter, room temperature

SASKATOON FILLING

6 cups fresh or frozen saskatoon berries

3 Tbsp water

3 Tbsp fresh lemon juice

1 cup granulated sugar

⅓ cup all-purpose flour

¼ tsp nutmeg

1 Tbsp cornstarch

rolling pin, roll the dough from the centre outward. While rolling out your dough, keep rotating it, lightly flouring the surface under the dough as well as the top as needed to prevent it from sticking. Roll the dough out to no more than ¼ inch thick.

Flip a 9-inch pie plate upside down onto the dough. Using a sharp knife, trace a circle 1 to 2 inches out from the edge of the pie plate. Fold the circle of dough in half and transfer it to the pie plate, making sure it's nicely centred. Unfold the dough, and then, using your fingers, gently press it down to form the pie shell, leaving the extra dough hanging over the edge of the pie plate. Working around the edge of the shell, snugly tuck the dough under itself, forming a thick rim around the edge of the plate. Using the thumb of one hand, press the dough between the thumb and forefinger of the other hand, forming a crimped peak. Freeze the shell for at least 15 minutes while you prepare the crumble topping and filling.

CRUMBLE TOPPING In a bowl, combine oats, flour, brown sugar, and cinnamon. Add butter and, using your hands, work it into the dry ingredients until large clumps form. Set aside.

SASKATOON FILLING Preheat your oven to 375°F.

In a large saucepan, combine saskatoons, water, lemon juice, and sugar. Cook on medium heat until sugar dissolves and mixture begins to simmer, about 5 minutes. Stir in flour, nutmeg, and cornstarch and continue to cook until mixture thickens, about 10 minutes.

TO ASSEMBLE Fill the pie shell to the rim with the saskatoon filling and top with crumb topping. Bake for 45 to 50 minutes, until the top is golden brown and the filling is bubbling. Serve pie slightly warm or allow it to cool completely. This pie will keep at room temperature for up to 3 days.

Filistix Mobile Kitchen

ARIEL DEL ROSARIO
▪ *chef* ▪

ROEL CANAFRANCA
▪ *chef* ▪

When Ariel del Rosario and his cousin Roel Canafranca (pictured left) launched Filistix— originally a Filipino-meat-on-a-stick food trailer on Rice Howard Way—it was Edmonton's first mobile eatery.

That was way back in 2008, during those dark days when Edmonton's street-food scene consisted of hot dogs and, well, hot dogs. The cousins' short-lived stint on that cobblestoned street has since grown into three busy locations: brick-and-mortar spots at University of Alberta and MacEwan University campuses, and their roaming trailer.

THE FILI-CHILI

With classic Filipino adobos (meat simmered in vinegar and soy, a remnant of Spanish colonialism) and homey South Pacific Coconut Curry Chicken, this dynamic duo has rescued many a student from a steady diet of instant noodles, soggy sandwiches, and vending machine fare. Ariel and Roel believe that what students eat affects how they think and feel. All their dishes are made from scratch, and that's why, in flavour and philosophy, Filistix is an antidote to the processed, corporate food found elsewhere on both campuses.

In either case, you're just a short LRT trip away from a delicious, homemade bowl of kimchi beef or spicy pork belly sisig. And summer wouldn't be summer in U of A's quad without Filistix's mobile enterprise dishing up tasty Thai curries and jerk chicken rice bowls with pineapple salsa (all in biodegradable wares). It's never too late to go back to school, right? Or at least for lunch.

4 chicken thighs (4 oz each), bone in, skin on
1 tsp salt, divided
1 tsp freshly ground black pepper, divided
1 Tbsp soy sauce
1 Tbsp canola oil
1 Tbsp minced garlic
1 Tbsp minced fresh ginger
1 Tbsp curry powder

½ tsp Thai red chili flakes
(or regular chili flakes)
½ tsp granulated sugar
1 bay leaf
1 can (14 oz) coconut milk
½ cup chicken stock
1 Tbsp roughly chopped cilantro

SERVES 4

South Pacific Coconut Curry Chicken

SPRINKLE chicken thighs with ½ tsp of the salt, ½ tsp of the pepper, and soy sauce and rub to incorporate.

Heat oil in a large saucepan on medium-high. Sear chicken thighs, skin-side down, for 2 minutes. Turn over and sear for another minute. You just want to crisp up the skin and add a bit of colour for now; you'll fully cook them later. Remove thighs from pan and set aside.

Place the same pan back on medium heat. Add garlic, ginger, curry powder, chili flakes, sugar, bay leaf, and the remaining ½ tsp salt and ½ tsp pepper to the pan. Sauté for about 1 minute to aromatize.

Raise the heat to high and add coconut milk and chicken stock. Return chicken thighs to the pan, skin-side up, and bring liquid to a boil. Reduce heat to medium-low, cover with a lid, and simmer for 10 to 15 minutes, until the chicken is fully cooked and the sauce thickens to a gravy-like consistency. Taste sauce and adjust seasoning with a pinch of salt and pepper if needed.

Place thighs in a serving dish and garnish with cilantro. Serve with a side of steamed fragrant jasmine rice and Filistix's signature Napa Cabbage Slaw (page 89).

1 **Tbsp** minced garlic
1 **Tbsp** Dijon mustard
2 **Tbsp** granulated sugar
¼ **cup** soy sauce
¼ **cup** balsamic vinegar
¼ **cup** sesame oil

2 **cups** canola oil
4 **cups** shredded napa cabbage
(about 1 small head)
1 **cup** shredded red cabbage
(about 1 small head)

4 **Tbsp** dried cranberries,
plus more for garnish
4 **Tbsp** sliced almonds,
plus more for garnish
1 **Tbsp** chopped green onions,
plus more for garnish

SERVES **4**

Napa Cabbage Slaw
with Sesame-Soy Balsamic Vinaigrette

IN A MEDIUM BOWL, combine garlic, mustard, sugar, soy sauce, balsamic vinegar, and sesame oil. Whisk until ingredients form a thin paste. Drizzle canola oil slowly into the bowl while whisking vigorously until dressing emulsifies. This process can also be done in a food processor, if preferred.

In a large bowl, combine napa and red cabbage and 1 to 1 ½ cups of dressing, according to your taste. Save the remaining dressing for another use; it will keep for a few weeks in the fridge.

Toss slaw gently, coating all of the cabbage leaves. Sprinkle with dried cranberries, almonds, and green onions and toss again. To serve, top with additional cranberries, almonds, and green onions.

ADOBO
THIGHS
STYLE ADOBO
GARLIC, SOY & CHILI
PACIFIC" COCONUT CHICKEN

The Hardware Grill

LARRY STEWART

▪ *chef* ▪

At a time when young, tattooed chefs are dishing small plates in Edison-light-bulbed rooms all over the city, the 20-year-old Hardware Grill remains a citadel of fine dining. It feels subversive, even defiant, to dine in this luxurious room in the historic Goodridge Block and indulge in French Canadian foie gras with bacon-stuffed chocolate French toast and maple-chipotle syrup, or crispy duck leg confit with cherry marmalade and straw potatoes. And those are just the starters.

Indeed, words like *bacon*, *lobster*, and *truffle* are sprinkled like confetti throughout chef Larry Stewart's seasonal menu of French and

Italian classics updated with bold, new-world flavours. You can sit at the chef's table in the kitchen for front-row action and a set five-course menu, or slip into a curved banquette and peruse the dinner menu and 19-page wine list, complete with a table of contents. Larry's *Wine Spectator* award-winning list is symbolic of his more-is-more approach. See, for example, his posh take on a cherished Prairie favourite: perogies. His are decadent, stuffed with truffled potatoes and fried in butter until golden, and arrive with an entourage of grainy-mustard cream sauce, smoked salmon, and (why hold back now?) salmon caviar.

For dessert, a large wedge of moist and comforting gingerbread cake so good it's been on the menu since day one. It, too, has an entourage: rhubarb-saskatoon compote, warm caramel sauce, and mango ice cream. Yes, it's all a bit rich (as is the crowd), but this is, after all, Edmonton fine dining at its best.

MUSTARD CREAM SAUCE

4 Tbsp butter
2 cups whipping (35%) cream
½ tsp salt
½ tsp freshly ground black pepper
2 tsp whey powder
½ cup grainy mustard

PEROGIES

1 cup all-purpose flour
1 ⅓ cup sour cream, divided
2 lbs red or white potatoes, skin on, quartered
½ cup butter
⅓ cup whipping (35%) cream
1 tsp salt
½ tsp freshly ground black pepper
1 Tbsp truffle peelings, coarsely chopped
1 tsp white truffle oil

ASSEMBLY

1 Tbsp butter
6 oz applewood smoked salmon, thinly sliced
4 tsp crème fraîche (or sour cream)
4 tsp Canadian salmon caviar
Chives, chopped, for garnish

SERVES **4**

Smoked Salmon
with Truffled Potato Perogies

MUSTARD CREAM SAUCE In a saucepan on medium heat, melt butter. Add cream and bring to a simmer. Add salt, pepper, whey powder, and mustard and whisk to combine. Pour into an air-tight container and place it in the fridge overnight.

Tip: The mustard cream sauce is best if made the day before.

PEROGIES Mix flour and 1 cup of the sour cream together thoroughly to form a smooth dough. Wrap in plastic wrap and refrigerate for at least 4 hours.

Cover potatoes with water in a large pot and boil until tender, 15 to 20 minutes. Drain thoroughly.

Mash potatoes and mix in butter, the remaining ⅓ cup sour cream, whipping cream, salt, and pepper. Mix well, then add truffle peelings and oil. Mix, taste, and adjust seasonings to your liking.

On a floured countertop, roll out chilled dough to about ⅜ inch thick. Cut out 2-inch circles using a cookie cutter or a pint glass. Dough should make 12 to 18 circles. Scoop about 2 Tbsp of the potato filling onto each circle. Fold dough over to form a crescent. Pinch edges together to ensure filling is well sealed.

Bring a large pot of water to a boil. Boil perogies in batches for about 5 minutes, or until they bob to the surface. Drain and rinse in cold water, then drain again and pat dry.

TO ASSEMBLE In a large sauté pan on medium heat, melt butter. Sauté perogies until they are golden brown.

On each plate dab 2 Tbsp mustard cream sauce and top with 2 or 3 perogies, 1½ oz smoked salmon, and a dollop of crème fraîche and caviar. Finish with a sprinkling of chives.

Perogies freeze well. Double or triple this recipe to have extras on hand. Lay the fresh perogies on a parchment-lined baking sheet and freeze them for a few hours before placing them in freezer bags. (This prevents the perogies from sticking to each other.) They keep for about 6 months in the freezer.

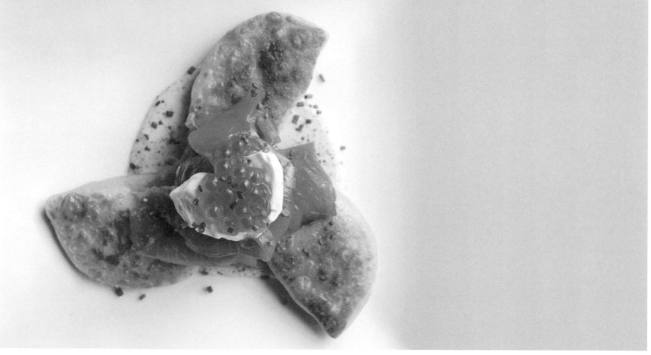

WARM GINGERBREAD
1 cup + 1 Tbsp boiling water
⅔ cup + 1 Tbsp fancy molasses
½ tsp baking soda
2 ⅔ cups all-purpose flour
2 ½ Tbsp baking powder
¼ tsp ground cloves
1 Tbsp ground ginger
1 Tbsp ground cinnamon
½ tsp salt

⅔ cup unsalted butter
¾ cup brown sugar, packed
1 egg

RHUBARB-SASKATOON COMPOTE
¾ cup frozen diced rhubarb
(½-inch pieces)
¾ cup frozen saskatoon berries
¾ cup granulated sugar
1 Tbsp water
2 Tbsp cornstarch

CARAMEL SAUCE
1 cup brown sugar, packed
½ cup unsalted butter
½ cup whipping (35%) cream
2 Tbsp orange juice concentrate
Salt

SERVES 6-8

Warm Gingerbread
with Caramel Sauce and Rhubarb-Saskatoon Compote

WARM GINGERBREAD Preheat the oven to 350°F. Grease a 9-inch cake pan and set aside.

Combine boiling water, molasses, and baking soda in a small saucepan and allow the mixture to cool.

In a large bowl, sift together flour, baking powder, cloves, ginger, cinnamon, and salt. Set aside.

In a large mixing bowl, cream butter and brown sugar until light and fluffy. Add egg and continue to mix. Scrape down the sides of the bowl and mix well.

Pour a third of the molasses mixture into the butter mixture and stir to combine. Next, add a third of the flour mixture and mix. Repeat until everything is combined into a smooth batter.

Pour batter into the cake pan and bake for about 1 hour. (While the cake bakes, make the compote and caramel sauce.) Test if the gingerbread is fully baked by sticking a skewer into the centre; if it comes out clean, the cake is done. Allow to cool to room temperature.

RHUBARB-SASKATOON COMPOTE Combine rhubarb, saskatoons, and sugar in a small pot. Cover with a lid and bring to a simmer on medium-low heat. In a small bowl, mix water and cornstarch into a slurry. Pour it into berry mixture, whisking thoroughly. Bring compote back to a simmer and cook until it becomes thick, smooth, and shiny, with no chalkiness. Allow it to cool.

CARAMEL SAUCE Combine brown sugar, butter, cream, orange juice concentrate, and a pinch of salt in a medium saucepan. Bring to a simmer on medium heat and cook for 30 minutes, until thick and glossy and smooth. Store in an airtight container at room temperature.

TO ASSEMBLE Warm cake in the oven or microwave (or keep it cold, according to your preference). Cut cake into 6 to 8 pieces. Warm caramel sauce on the stove and ladle 2 Tbsp on each piece. Garnish with 1 to 2 Tbsp of compote. Serve with mango or vanilla ice cream, as desired.

Izakaya Tomo

TOMOYA MUTAGUCHI

▪ *chef* ▪

When Tomoya Mutaguchi decided to open a Japanese restaurant back in 2012, he knew he didn't want to offer the homogenous sushi-tempura-teriyaki concept common in Edmonton strip malls and food courts. Instead, he opened the city's first izakaya—Japan's take on tapas bars, with emphasis on the bar—a friendly watering hole where you can kick back over a drink (or three) and small plates to share.

Although izakaya food is bar food, in quintessential Japanese style, it's exquisitely refined and impeccably balanced, especially so here. No wonder Izakaya Tomo, open late and perpetually packed, is where the city's best chefs

eat on their days off, bingeing on crispy chicken skin with ponzu sauce and Carbonara Udon.

Grab a seat at one of the picnic-style tables and plan to linger over beer, sake, plum wine, shochu (a distilled spirit), or Japanese single-malt whisky (yes, it exists, and it's mellow and caramelly). You'll want to order one of something raw, fried, pickled, and simmered, all beautifully plated on stoneware that reinforces the restaurant's rustic yet minimalist, clean-lined aesthetic.

For something raw, the kimchi tuna tartare is luscious and zingy, topped with sesame seeds and feral rings of scallions. The Tonpei

Yaki, typically eaten in Osaka, is Mutaguchi's signature dish: an omelette stuffed with savoury shaved pork and strands of sake-soaked cabbage, topped with sweet-salty okonomiyaki sauce, creamy Japanese mayo, and ethereal bonito flakes that dance on top like a welcome greeting. As you leave, the staff will shout *"Arigatou gozaimashita"* to thank you for your patronage. Commit those words to memory, why don't you? Because you'll find yourself wanting to thank them right back.

32 oz udon noodles
1 Tbsp extra-virgin olive oil
12 oz bacon, cut into ¾-inch strips
1 large onion, chopped
4 cloves garlic, minced
4 tsp freshly ground black pepper

2 cups light (10%) cream
¼ cup finely grated Parmigiano Reggiano,
divided, plus more for garnish
4 egg yolks
Salt
2 Tbsp finely chopped parsley

SERVES 4

Carbonara Udon

COOK udon noodles according to package instructions, or in boiling water for 5 minutes. Drain and set aside.

Heat oil in a frying pan on medium. Add bacon and sauté until it begins to get crispy, 2 to 5 minutes. Add onions, garlic, and pepper and sauté until bacon is fully crisp.

Add cream and bring to a boil. Reduce heat and simmer until liquid thickens, about 2 minutes.

Add cooked udon and half of the Parmigiano Reggiano to the pan.

Whisk egg yolks in a small bowl.

Remove the pan from the heat. Add egg yolks and remaining Parmigiano Reggiano. Working as quickly as you can, toss noodles and sauce around the pan until noodles are coated. Adjust seasoning with salt and pepper to taste.

TO SERVE Divide noodles among 4 bowls. Sprinkle each dish with a little more Parmigiano Reggiano, parsley, and freshly cracked pepper.

½ **cup** ketchup
¼ **cup** Worcestershire sauce
3 Tbsp honey

PORK AND CABBAGE

3–4 Tbsp vegetable oil, divided
1 lb pork shoulder, sliced into thin strips
4 cups thinly shredded cabbage
Salt and freshly ground black pepper
½ cup sake

ASSEMBLY

2–3 Tbsp vegetable oil, divided
8 eggs
½ cup Japanese mayonnaise
1 ½ oz bonito flakes

SERVES **4**

Tonpei Yaki

OKONOMIYAKI SAUCE In a small bowl, stir together all ingredients until well combined.

PORK AND CABBAGE Heat 2 Tbsp of the oil in a wok or frying pan on medium-high, and stir-fry pork until the meat is no longer pink, 6 to 8 minutes. Set aside.

Stir-fry shredded cabbage and prepared pork on a frying pan or griddle on medium heat. If using a frying pan, add another 1 Tbsp of oil to fry. Add a sprinkling of salt and pepper and the sake. Cover for 3 to 4 minutes until the cabbage is wilted. Remove the cabbage and pork mixture from the griddle or frying pan and set aside.

TO ASSEMBLE Heat 1 Tbsp of the vegetable oil in a non-stick pan on medium.

In a bowl, whisk 2 eggs. Pour eggs into the pan and tilt the pan around until egg coats the bottom completely. Add a quarter of the cabbage and pork mixture and, once eggs are mostly cooked with a bit still wet, about 3 minutes, roll the eggs like an omelette so that filling is secure inside. Set the roll aside. Add more oil to the pan as needed and repeat with remaining eggs and cabbage and pork mixture.

To serve, drizzle each roll generously with okonomiyaki sauce, Japanese mayonnaise, and a sprinkling of bonito flakes.

Tip: You can find Japanese mayonnaise at many supermarkets and Asian specialty markets.

JACEK Chocolate Couture

JACQUELINE JACEK
· owner ·

Every four months Jacqueline Jacek, Edmonton's self-proclaimed Cocoanista, designs a limited collection of six chocolates. A hush falls when it's time to open one of her Tiffany-blue and cocoa–hued boxes, as if a great treasure is about to be revealed. And treasures there are: glossy, hand-painted shells with a crisp snap that give way to pristine bites of chocolate silk, otherwise known as ganache, that melt in your mouth.

Jacqueline's Mad Hatter's Collection was inspired by *Alice in Wonderland*. There was the brilliant Sage and Smoked Chanterelle Truffle (caramelized white chocolate with sage

topped with smoked local chanterelle ganache) and Unbirthday Cake (a milk chocolate layer over vanilla bean ganache all dressed in dark chocolate).

Like many perfectionist gastronomes, Jacqueline is selective about her ingredients. She uses Valrhona and Cacao Barry chocolate made with cocoa beans sourced from Madagascar and Peru and blends different types to create chocolates with bright, acidic notes that are also deep and full of character. Jacqueline began making chocolates in her home and selling them at farmers' markets in 2009. A 2,100-square-foot facility and retail shop followed two years later, and most recently, a second location—a Parisian industrial-chic boutique on 104 Street. Thick, dark sipping chocolate, chocolate-covered nuts, and a Fabric Collection—Jacqueline's inaugural bean-to-bar collection made using ethically sourced cocoa beans that she sorts, roasts, winnows, and refines in-house—round out her in-store offerings.

Drop by the next time you feel like treating a special someone—especially if that someone is you.

1 cup Valrhona Manjari 64% chocolate, finely chopped (or use the highest-quality dark chocolate you can find)

½ cup whipping (35%) cream
1 Tbsp light corn syrup
1 Tbsp unsalted butter, room temperature
¼ cup Valrhona cocoa powder

MAKES **30** *truffles*

Classic Dark Chocolate Truffles

PLACE chopped chocolate in a heatproof bowl.

In a saucepan on medium heat, warm cream and corn syrup. Bring the cream and syrup to 176°F, or just to the point before it boils.

Pour cream mixture over chopped chocolate and allow to sit for 1 minute.

Using a spatula and working in small circles, stir cream and chocolate slowly and carefully, starting in the centre and working your way to the outside until incorporated. The mixture should be smooth and shiny.

Add butter and use an immersion blender to fully incorporate.

Allow the mixture to cool to 77°F (measure if you can, or just guess; 77°F is a little warmer than room temperature). Use the immersion blender once more to get the smoothest truffles possible, 1 to 2 minutes.

Place the bowl in the fridge to cool mixture until firm. It should take about 20 minutes.

Fill a shallow bowl or pie plate with cocoa powder. Once the truffle mixture is firm, scoop out 1-Tbsp pieces and, using your hands, roll into balls. Roll the balls in cocoa powder to finish. Serve immediately or keep refrigerated until needed. Keep them in the fridge for 1 week, or freeze in an airtight container for up to 3 months.

Tip: Truffles can be rolled in all kinds of things, like coconut or crushed nuts. If serving to guests, let everyone roll their own truffles for an added bit of fun.

1 ½ cups granulated sugar

MILK CHOCOLATE SHELL
4 cups of Cacao Barry Lactée Supérieure, or any fine-quality milk chocolate wafers or melts

GANACHE
¾ cup Cacao Barry Lactée Supérieure, or any fine-quality milk chocolate wafers or melts
½ cup whipping (35%) cream
5 Tbsp burnt caramel powder
⅛ tsp fine sea salt
2 Tbsp unsalted butter, room temperature

ASSEMBLY
Edible shimmer powder in Inca Gold (available at Barb's Kitchen Centre and bakery supply shops)

MAKES **40** *truffles*

Salted Burnt Caramel Truffles

Making candy is an adventure! It's not difficult, but it does require careful attention to detail and instructions. Be brave and you'll be thrilled with the outcome. For the best results with these truffles, get yourself a digital thermometer, a silicone baking mat, an offset spatula, a polycarbonate mould (available at fine kitchen supply stores), and a fresh, small paint brush.

BURNT CARAMEL POWDER Set out a baking sheet lined with a silicone pad. If you don't have a silicone pad, you can line the baking sheet with parchment (but the pad makes cleanup easier!).

In a wide saucepan on medium to high heat, cook sugar until it turns a very dark molasses colour and starts to smoke a little, about 5 minutes. Remove from the heat and pour sugar carefully onto the baking sheet and allow it to cool.

Once completely cooled, the mixture will be very brittle and hard. Break it up into pieces with your hands. Place pieces into a food processor and process into a fine powder. Set aside.

MILK CHOCOLATE SHELL In a heatproof bowl over a pot of gently simmering water (or in the top of a double boiler), melt roughly 2 ½ cups of the chocolate. Clip your digital thermometer to the side of the bowl. When chocolate reaches 113°F, remove the bowl from the heat and wipe the outside with a cloth to ensure there is no water. Water is like poison for chocolate: it will cause the chocolate to seize, and the texture will be ruined.

Stirring constantly, add ½ cup (about one-third) of the remaining unmelted chocolate into the melted chocolate. Continue adding small amounts slowly, stirring to help it melt, until the thermometer reads 86°F (you may not need to use all of the pieces). Remove any unmelted pieces from the chocolate and set aside in a bowl for later use. Your chocolate is now tempered.

Set out a baking sheet on the counter and place polycarbonate mould on the baking sheet. Pour the tempered chocolate into the mould, then bang the mould on the counter a few times to remove any air bubbles.

Tip: Ensure your mould has 40 shell spaces, or have multiple moulds on hand.

Working over the baking sheet, flip the mould over, tapping the side gently with the handle of an offset spatula to knock out excess chocolate. This will cover the mould in chocolate and create a shell. Turn the mould right-side up again, and, scraping away from you, use the offset spatula to remove excess chocolate from the top. Place the mould in the fridge for about 15 minutes to set (shells will release from mould easily once set).

With a rubber spatula, scrape the excess chocolate off of the baking sheet into a bowl. You will use it when assembling the final chocolates.

GANACHE Place chocolate pieces in a heat-proof bowl.

To a pot on medium-low heat, add cream, burnt caramel powder, and sea salt. Stir quickly to make sure caramel powder dissolves. Clip a digital thermometer to the side and heat until mixture reaches 176°F.

Remove hot cream mixture from the heat and pour over the chocolate. Allow it to sit for 1 minute.

Using a spatula and working in small circles, stir cream and chocolate together, starting in the centre and working your way to the outside. Once the mixture has cooled to 100°F, add butter. Using an immersion blender, mix until butter is incorporated. Allow it to cool to 86°F.

Using a piping bag or a plastic bag with the corner snipped off, pipe ganache into prepared chocolate shells until 90 percent filled. Allow filled shells to sit at room temperature overnight.

ASSEMBLY It's time to reuse your tempered chocolate! Chop up chocolate saved when you made the shells, and melt about one-third of it. Repeat the tempering method used for making the shells: Clip your digital thermometer to the side of the bowl. When chocolate reaches 113°F, remove the bowl from the heat and wipe the outside with a cloth to ensure there is no water.

Stirring constantly, add ½ cup of the remaining unmelted chocolate into the melted chocolate. Continue adding small amounts slowly, stirring to help it melt, until the thermometer reads 86°F.

Pour a small amount of chocolate over the filled shells. Starting at the end closest to you, and using your offset spatula, gently "push" the chocolate over the shells and away from you, making sure there are no air bubbles or holes (this is the "seal" for the truffles). Place in the fridge for 5 minutes.

Remove from the fridge and gently turn over mould to knock out the filled chocolates. Using a small, clean paintbrush, finish chocolates by applying a thin coating of edible shimmer powder. Store chocolates at room temperature. They will keep for 2 weeks.

Langano Skies

AMSALE SUMAMO

chef

At the heart of Langano Skies is Amsale—her food, her warmth, her welcoming spirit, and, of course, her inviting smile. But we might never have experienced any of these things were it not for Paul, her husband and business partner.

In 2004, Langano Skies became Edmonton's newest restaurant featuring Ethiopian cuisine, opening on the quieter eastern end of Whyte Avenue. But Paul's campaign to convince Amsale to open a restaurant actually began some 15 years earlier; it started with the purchase of tablecloths and artwork from Ethiopia for the restaurant—talk about confidence and perseverance!

After a few bites of spice-laced lentils or tender stir-fried chicken and vegetables, scooped up with fresh *injera* (the ubiquitous sourdough flatbread Amsale makes fresh daily), you'll understand why Paul never gave up. Amsale's food—including the popular monthly vegan buffet—is the perfect example of the best of Ethiopia and yet uniquely her own. Don't bother asking her for the recipe for *nitir kibeh*, her spice-infused clarified butter; she's taking that to her grave.

Amsale was raised on a farm in northern Ethiopia among papaya, banana, and coffee trees, so perhaps it's no surprise that cooking has always come as naturally to her as breathing. Langano Skies is a family restaurant, with wife, husband, and adult children Elizabeth, Yonathan, Simon, and Salome all playing a vital role. There is joy in Amsale's food. You can feel it when you walk in. You can see it in the faces of the happy regulars who call the restaurant their home away from home. And, of course, you can taste it in every single dish.

1 large onion, puréed in food processor

¼ cup vegetable oil

3–4 cups water, divided

4 cloves garlic, puréed in food processor

2 lbs chopped frozen spinach, thawed

1 Tbsp salt

SERVES 6

Gomen Wot
(*Spinach Stew*)

ADD onion to a large, cold pot on the stovetop and bring heat up to medium-low. Cover the pot with a lid, stirring occasionally. Be sure not to brown the onions—just sweat them, for about 5 minutes. Because they are puréed, they will release a lot more juice than chopped onions. Add vegetable oil and 1 cup of the water. Stir and continue to cook, uncovered, for about 10 minutes, until onions become golden brown and separate from the oil. Stir occasionally to make sure onions don't burn.

Add garlic and cook for another 5 minutes, stirring occasionally to keep the mixture from sticking to the pot.

Add spinach (don't drain the water) to the pot and stir. Cook for about 25 minutes, until creamy and smooth. Add water as needed to keep the mixture moist and creamy, about 2 cups total. Keep the spinach just covered with water for about 15 minutes, and then let the water cook off for the last 10 minutes. Do not let the spinach dry out and stick to the pot; it should be a smooth, stew-like consistency. Add salt, then taste and adjust seasoning as needed.

Traditionally this stew is served with injera, *but it also goes well with rice, pita, potatoes, or roti. Serve alongside Yemisir Kik Wot (page 114) for a complete vegetarian meal.*

1 cup red lentils (masoor daal)
1 large onion, puréed in food processor
¼ cup vegetable oil
5 cups water, divided
3–4 cloves garlic, puréed in food processor

3 Tbsp berbere
2 Tbsp tomato paste
1 Tbsp salt
(less if you have a very salty berbere; adjust to taste)

SERVES 6

Yemisir Kik Wot
(*Red Lentils*)

Berbere (pronounced "berrberré") is an Ethiopian spice blend made up of sun-dried red chilies, garlic, ginger, allspice, cardamom, and salt. Look for it in supermarkets or South Asian grocery stores, or order it online. Each blend is different, and yours may be more spicy or milder than the one used at Langano Skies, so consider how spicy you want your lentils to be before you add the full amount indicated here.

RINSE lentils in a colander 3 to 4 times until the water runs clear. Once lentils are clean, cover them with water and allow them to soak for 30 minutes. They should double in size.

Add onions to a large, cold pot on the stovetop and bring heat up to medium-low. Cover the pot with a lid, stirring occasionally. Be sure not to brown the onions — just sweat them, for about 5 minutes. Because they are puréed, they will release a lot more juice than chopped onions. Add vegetable oil and 1 cup of the water. Stir and continue to cook, uncovered, for about 10 minutes, until onions become golden brown and separate from oil. Stir occasionally to make sure onions don't burn.

Add garlic and cook for another 5 minutes, stirring occasionally to keep mixture from sticking to the pot.

Add berbere and tomato paste and stir. Add 1 cup of the water and cook for 10 minutes on medium-low heat.

Drain the water from the lentils and add them to the pot along with the remaining 3 cups water. (If you like a thick stew, consider adding less water at this stage.)

Turn up heat and bring lentils to a boil. Once they are boiling, turn heat down to low and let lentils cook, covered, until they are soft, 25 to 30 minutes. Check occasionally to see if stew requires more water.

Add salt. Taste and adjust seasoning, as desired.

Traditionally, this stew is served with injera, but it also goes well with rice, pita, potatoes, or roti. Serve alongside Gomen Wot (page 113) for a complete vegetarian meal.

Little Brick

NATE BOX
▪ *owner* ▪

CHAEL MACDONALD
▪ *chef at Little Brick* ▪

ERICA VLIEGENTHART
▪ *pastry chef* ▪

ALLAN SUDDABY
▪ *head chef* ▪

Sure, setting up a restaurant in a 1903 home in a residential neighbourhood might seem like a bad idea. But when you sit on the backyard patio sipping a perfect cappuccino as the sun emerges from behind a cloud, it's perfectly clear why Little Brick succeeds. Because it's awesome. Who doesn't secretly want to eat delicious food in their backyard with their neighbours and friends?

The fourth café from Nate Box (far left), Little Brick is, in some ways, the culmination of the others. It includes the standard tasty coffee drinks, delicious sandwiches, and baked goods, but also introduces a general store stocked

with curated local favourites, an upstairs office space, and the aforementioned backyard with picnic tables and room for grilling and live music. Box's café empire began with Elm Café in 2010, a tiny space under an office building in Oliver, selling quality coffee and sandwiches to condo dwellers on the go. With this first success, and a growing catering wing helmed by talented chef Allan Suddaby (far right), District Coffee was born the year after when a space further downtown became available. Next came Burrow Grab and Go Café, a kiosk in the Central LRT station slinging coffee, baked goods, breakfast, and lunches to commuters.

Box and his team just can't pass up the challenge of taking underused space and turning it into a delicious oasis. But it takes a team, and Little Brick, like the others, is the product of collaboration, with chef Chael MacDonald (second from left) taking the leading role. The recipes shared here reflect interdependence. We have Allan's comforting Country Chicken Stew, head baker Erica's badass pastry technique with the biscuits, Chael's smart no-waste policy in the dressing, and Nate's approachability in the salad. All together, great.

¼ **cup** unsalted butter

1 ½ cups chopped yellow onions

2 cloves garlic, minced

1 Tbsp sweet paprika

1 Tbsp dried oregano

¼ **cup** dry white wine

1 cup chopped carrots

1 cup chopped celery

1 ½ cups chopped red pepper

4 cups chopped Yukon gold potatoes

1 cup chopped summer squash

½ **cup** corn kernels, fresh or frozen

4 cups chicken stock

1 lb cooked chicken, preferably legs,

shredded or cut into chunks

⅓ **cup** chopped fresh herbs
(a mixture of parsley, thyme,
rosemary, and sage)

1 Tbsp white wine vinegar
Kosher salt and freshly ground
black pepper

MAKES **10** *cups of stew +* **9** *biscuits*

Country Chicken Stew and Biscuits

CHICKEN STEW In a heavy-bottomed pot on medium heat, melt butter. Add onions, garlic, paprika, and oregano and cook until onions start to turn translucent, about 10 minutes. Add white wine and simmer until liquid reduces by about one-third.

Add carrots, celery, red peppers, potatoes, squash, and corn. Add chicken stock until vegetables are just covered (you may not need all 4 cups). Bring to a simmer and turn down heat to medium-low. Allow the stew to simmer until vegetables are tender, 10 to 15 minutes (the potatoes will take the longest). Remove from the heat.

Transfer 2 cups of the stew into a blender, allow it to cool, and blend into a smooth purée. Add purée back into stew and stir to combine. This will make it thick and luscious.

Add chicken, herbs, and vinegar. Return pot to a gentle simmer. Adjust seasoning with salt and pepper to taste.

Tip: Chop all the vegetables into ¾-inch pieces or to your taste. Try to keep them relatively uniform so that they cook evenly.

FLAKY BUTTERMILK BISCUITS

3 cups all-purpose flour
1 Tbsp baking powder
1 tsp baking soda
1 ½ tsp salt
1 ⅓ cups unsalted butter, cold, diced (½-inch cubes)
1 ¼ cups buttermilk
¼ cup melted butter, for brushing

FLAKY BUTTERMILK BISCUITS Preheat the oven to 380°F and line a baking sheet with parchment paper.

In a large bowl, combine flour, baking powder, baking soda, and salt. Whisk together.

Using your hands, which should be cold for this step, work butter into dry mixture until it turns into small flattened bits the size of peas. Add buttermilk in thirds, fluffing with your hands to gently combine. Be sure to add the buttermilk slowly to evenly hydrate mixture and avoid making dry patches or wet clumps.

Turn the mixture out onto a clean surface and gently press into a rectangle with your hands. Tidy the borders and gently press and roll into an 8 × 12-inch rectangle. Don't worry if the dough is a little shaggy. Cut dough into thirds of about 8 × 4 inches.

Stack the thirds on top of each other to create layers. Using a rolling pin, gently roll dough back into an 8 × 12-inch piece and repeat the layering step once more. (This is how you achieve flakiness.)

Once you have layered your dough twice, roll it out to a 10 × 10-inch square. Use a 3-inch ring cutter to punch out 9 biscuits. If you don't have a ring mould, you can use a pint glass. Be sure to push the cutter straight up and down, and do not twist or turn. Twisting your cutter can mess up your layers and result in distorted biscuits.

Place biscuits on baking sheet and brush the tops lightly with melted butter. Bake for about 10 minutes or until golden brown. Biscuits are at their best straight out of the oven, but if you have leftovers, allow them to cool and store them in an airtight container.

TO ASSEMBLE Serve the chicken stew in bowls, with a flaky biscuit on the side for dunking.

FRESH RICOTTA

4 cups whole milk
1 cup buttermilk
Kosher salt
Apple cider vinegar,
to taste

FRESH TOMATO VINAIGRETTE

1 cup tomato ends and tomato water
(or just chopped tomatoes)
½ tsp salt
1 tsp honey
1 Tbsp apple cider vinegar
(McKernan brand or any high-quality
or local variety)
¼ tsp fresh thyme leaves
1 Tbsp cold-pressed canola oil
2 Tbsp regular canola oil

TOMATO SALAD

4 cups hearty greens (e.g., kale, sorrel)
4 cups leaf lettuce
½ cup flat-leaf parsley leaves
8 vine tomatoes, preferably yellow
24–32 cherry or grape tomatoes, preferably zebra
2 cups sprouts (e.g., pea, chickpea, alfalfa, broccoli)
4 medium carrots, cut paper thin or into ribbons
½ cup fresh tomato vinaigrette, or to taste
1 cup fresh ricotta
Maldon salt and freshly ground black pepper

SERVES **4**

Tomato Salad
with Fresh Ricotta

FRESH RICOTTA In a heavy-bottomed stainless steel pot, combine milk and buttermilk and gently warm on medium-low heat. As the milk warms, occasionally scrape the bottom of the pot with a rubber spatula.

When the milk hits about 176°F, it will split into curds and whey. When this happens, remove the pot from the heat and allow it to stand for at least 15 minutes.

While the milk cools, hook a fine-mesh strainer over a bowl large enough to hold the whey (the liquid) in your ricotta mixture without overflowing. Gently pour curds into the strainer over the bowl and allow to drip for at least 1 hour. Ideally, leave the bowl in the fridge overnight. You can discard the whey, but why waste it when you can use it multiple ways — to braise a pork shoulder, for example, or in your next cream-base soup.

Pour curds into a food processor or blender, or simply break them up by hand until you achieve your desired consistency. The more you process, the more creamy the cheese will be. Be careful not to overprocess or the cheese will become too dry.

Season to taste with kosher salt and a splash of cider vinegar. Label, date, and refrigerate — or eat right away! (The leftovers will keep for a few days in the fridge.)

FRESH TOMATO VINAIGRETTE Place tomato ends, tomato water, salt, honey, vinegar, and thyme in a blender or food processor. Blend on high until completely smooth, about 1 minute. While the blender is still running, add canola oil in an even stream over a span of 30 to 40 seconds, until emulsified.

Pour the mixture through a fine-mesh strainer, using a ladle or a spoon to push through all of the liquid, leaving only dry pulp in the strainer. This recipe makes about 1 cup, which is more than you need for the salad. Transfer liquid to a squeeze bottle or set aside in a bowl for immediate use. Always shake the bottle to remix before use.

TOMATO SALAD Combine greens, lettuce, parsley, tomatoes, sprouts, and carrots in a large bowl and toss with vinaigrette. Toss and add more vinaigrette as desired. Serve salad in 4 big bowls, topped with ricotta and sprinkled with salt and pepper to taste.

At Little Brick, the kitchen staff live the "waste not, want not" rule. When cutting tomatoes for sandwiches, salads, and other uses, the ends are saved, along with any tomato water that drips out onto the board while cutting. Once enough leftovers accumulate, it's time to make Chael MacDonald's fresh tomato vinaigrette.

Little Village

THEO PSALIOS
chef & owner

It was inevitable that Theo Psalios — the one-man operation behind Little Village Food Truck — would end up in the family restaurant business, despite his staunch rebellions. "I thought it was a life-sucker — all work, no play," says Theo. "That's the narrative I created for myself as the reason not to do this."

The Psalios name is synonymous with Greek food in Edmonton. Theo's family has owned a dozen restaurants since 1980, dishing up savoury moussaka, dolmades, and plenty of ouzo. In his heyday, the Psalios patriarch, Yianni Psalios, owned Koutouki, Yiannis on Whyte Avenue, and its sultry basement den, where the

Oilers used to hang out. Mark Messier had the keys to close up. And then there's the story of Theo's sister waking up with the Stanley Cup. Ask him to tell you; it's a good one.

After years of resisting, Theo gave in and agreed to head up Koutouki Ouzeri in the west end. And for two years, the innards of his family and restaurant life — fights with his dad, his sister's big, Greek wedding in Cyprus, and his own marriage proposal — were all laid bare for the insatiable Food Network viewers of his reality TV show.

When his father moved to Palm Springs a few years ago, Theo sold his restaurant and embraced the freedom a kitchen on wheels offers — to cater, to interact with customers, and to lead a balanced family life raising his three children. These days, you can find Theo in his blue and white truck on 108 Street, serving delicious renditions of roadside Greek souvlaki favourites. Take the cheekily named Lambwich — juicy lamb, slow roasted (with bone in for flavour), with minted yogurt, and pickled onions and cabbage; it's happiness tucked into a brioche bun. Theo, it seems, has taken more than a first-class menu on the road; he's also brought along his exacting standards — the mark of a great chef and restaurateur who's doing it his way.

LAMB

1 lamb shoulder (4–5 lbs), bone-in
½ cup extra-virgin olive oil
4 Tbsp Dijon mustard
Pinch of dried rosemary
Pinch of dried oregano
Salt and freshly ground black pepper
1 cup of water
Ingredients continued overleaf

SERVES 8

Lambwich
with Mint Yogurt and Pickled Onions and Cabbage

Ever since a foodie friend turned me on to Theo's lambwich, I haven't been able to try much else on Theo's menu; I love it that much. Luckily, Theo says he turns the roasted lamb from this sandwich into a main by serving it with the minted yogurt and a side of his legendary lemon-roasted potatoes (page 127). That's lunch and dinner, all wrapped up from one glorious roast.— **TF**

LAMB Preheat the oven to 275°F.

Rinse lamb shoulder with cold water, pat dry, and place, bone-side down, into a roasting pan. If using frozen lamb, be sure lamb is fully thawed before roasting.

Mix olive oil and mustard in a small bowl and pour over lamb. Sprinkle with rosemary, oregano, and a pinch of salt and pepper. Add water to the bottom of the pan.

Cover the pan with a lid or aluminum foil and cook for 7 hours or until meat falls effortlessly off the bone. For the best colour on the meat, remove the lid and roast for another 30 minutes.

Allow the lamb to rest for 1 hour or until it's cool enough to handle. Separate all of the meat from the fat and bones, using either your hands or a pair of forks. Either discard the bones or save them for another use (like making stock). They will keep in the freezer for up to a month. Taste the meat and season with more salt if needed.

Tip: Roasted lamb can be made up to 3 days ahead of time. Simply reheat when ready to assemble the sandwich.

Recipe continued overleaf

MINT YOGURT
2 cups fresh mint leaves, tightly packed
2 cups non-fat yogurt containing cornstarch

PICKLED ONIONS AND CABBAGE
4 Tbsp granulated sugar
2 Tbsp salt
1 cup red wine vinegar
1 cup water
½ red cabbage, finely sliced
2 red onions, finely sliced

ASSEMBLY
8 brioche buns
(or whichever type you prefer)

MINT YOGURT Place ingredients in a blender and mix until mint leaves have fully blended into yogurt. Cover and place in the fridge. The freshly blended mint will oxidize fairly quickly and create a brownish colour on the surface, so if you don't intend to use the yogurt right away, apply a piece of plastic wrap directly to the surface to keep browning to a minimum.

Tip: You need to use yogurt containing cornstarch here because it stays thick after blending, unlike a full-fat yogurt, which will break down during blending, leaving a runny mess.

PICKLED ONIONS AND CABBAGE In a small bowl, combine sugar, salt, vinegar, and water. Stir until sugar and salt are fully dissolved.

Place the cabbage and onions in a large glass jar, ideally a 4-cup Mason jar. Pour the vinegar mixture over the cabbage and cover with a lid or plastic wrap. (You can leave the jar in the fridge for 3 to 5 days, until you're ready to use it.)

TO ASSEMBLE Reheat lamb. You can use the oven, the microwave, or a frying pan — just make sure the meat is warmed through. Once the lamb is hot, lightly toast buns. Lay out bun bottoms and add a dollop of mint yogurt to each. Gently spoon the lamb on top of the yogurt, dividing evenly among the 8 buns. Top each with about ¼ cup pickled onions and cabbage. Add the bun tops and serve.

¼ **cup** salted butter, melted
⅓ **cup** chicken soup mix (without MSG)
1 tsp freshly ground black pepper
Juice of 2 lemons
⅔ **cup** canola oil

¼ onion, peeled
3 lbs new potatoes
(or any small potatoes, preferably
Yukon gold or red varieties),
skin on, halved

SERVES **6-8**

Lemon Roasted Potatoes

In all the years Theo's family has owned Greek restaurants, all anyone has ever wanted to know was how to make their tender, lemony potatoes. Theo happily admits the low-brow ingredient that makes them so satisfyingly savoury: regular ol' chicken soup mix. "It's junky, I know, but that's how they're made." And a little goes a long way.

PREHEAT the oven to 425°F.

In a medium bowl, mix butter, soup mix, pepper, lemon juice, and oil.

Lay onion and potatoes in a roasting pan large enough so that the potatoes make up no more than two layers (this will ensure they cook evenly and the skins get crispy). Top with the butter mixture, making sure the onion and potatoes are completely coated.

Roast potatoes for 50 to 60 minutes. If they seem to be browning too quickly on top, remove the pan from the oven and stir potatoes to bring the bottom layer to the top. Potatoes are finished when a fork goes through easily.

MEAT

NATHAN MCLAUGHLIN
• *chef & co-owner* •

A few steps away from the bustle of Whyte Avenue, a retro sign with a finger pointing boldly says "EAT MEAT HERE," and that's exactly what you'll do 'round the corner at MEAT.

Inside, MEAT's Scandinavian minimalist aesthetic welcomes you with blond wood communal tables, a wall of stacked firewood logs, and the warm smell of comfort food done right.

The concept here is authentic Texas-style barbecue: brisket, beer, and bourbon. It's a tasty alliteration made possible by a massive smoker imported from the USA. It can handle 700 pounds of meat and uses a combo of hickory and cherry wood to dispense mounds

of succulent brisket, delicious pulled pork, barbecue ribs, and juicy brined chicken.

Before opening MEAT in 2014, chef and co-owner Nathan McLaughlin spent a week eating in Austin, Texas, and another in Georgia training with Myron Mixon, three-time Grand Champion in the Memphis World Championship Barbecue Cooking Contest. Of all the barbecue on MEAT's menu, brisket is the hardest to master. But when cooked with patience and a deft hand, as Nathan's is, it's transformed into juicy, supple bites.

Food here is served on no-nonsense aluminum trays, a practical catch-all for the messy aftermath. Four house-made sauces are within reach on every table to dip or drench, as you like: cherry, spicy, mustard, and MEAT's signature bourbon, a molassesy-tangy concoction imbued with a spicy hum of chili, cayenne, and cumin. All you need to top things off is a cold craft brew, which can be enjoyed with a one-ounce shot of bourbon, a pairing known as a boilermaker. Why pick your poison when you can have both?

BRINED CHICKEN
1 chicken (2 ½–3 lbs)
½ cup granulated sugar
1 cup kosher salt
1 cup apple juice
16 cups cold water

RUB
4 tsp granulated sugar
4 tsp paprika
4 tsp onion powder
4 tsp mustard powder
4 tsp freshly ground black pepper

2 tsp dried oregano
1 ½ tsp kosher salt
1 ½ tsp garlic powder
1 tsp chili powder
1 tsp ground cumin

SERVES **2-3**

Smoked Chicken

The real secret to good barbecue is low and slow. Since this chicken achieves its succulence through a good long soak in a brine, be sure to start it the day before you plan to serve it. If you don't have a smoker, use the oven-roasting method for a juicy, moist bird without the smoke. Use the chicken on sandwiches, over salad, or as part of a platter. It tastes great with Bourbon BBQ sauce (page 132).

BRINED CHICKEN Thoroughly rinse chicken with cold water. Pat dry.

In a large, deep bowl or pot, stir together sugar, salt, apple juice, and water until fully dissolved. Place chicken in brine, making sure it is fully submerged. If it's not submerged, mix up a few more cups of brine at a ratio of 1 Tbsp of salt and ½ Tbsp of sugar per 1 cup water. Cover and leave in fridge for 12 to 24 hours.

RUB Combine all ingredients in a small bowl.

TO ASSEMBLE When ready to cook, remove chicken from the brine and pat dry with a paper towel, making sure to dry the inside of the cavity. Place chicken onto a baking sheet with a rack, and put it back in the fridge to air dry for 1 hour.

Preheat the oven to 350°F or the smoker to 220°F.

Remove chicken from the fridge and generously apply rub. Make sure you coat all of the skin and the inner cavity. You may place fresh herbs, lemon slices, or even butter in the cavity if you like.

SMOKER INSTRUCTIONS Place chicken in the smoker and cover with a lid. Cook for 4 hours, and maintain heat by adding more wood as needed. Place a thermometer in the thickest part of the thigh. When the internal temperature reaches 165°F, the chicken is done. Remove chicken from the smoker and allow it to rest for at least 20 minutes. Carve and serve.

OVEN INSTRUCTIONS Place chicken uncovered in the oven for 1 ½ hours. Cook until internal temperature reaches 165°F, then broil at 400°F for 5 to 7 minutes to crisp up the skin. Allow it to rest for at least 20 minutes before carving.

For smoking, MEAT uses cherry and hickory, but you can use whatever you like. Just make sure you are aware of the type of wood you are using, as some have stronger flavours and others are sweet.

3 Tbsp vegetable oil
½ cup chopped onions
¼ cup minced garlic
1 Tbsp chili powder
½ Tbsp ground cumin
½ Tbsp cayenne
¼ cup beef stock

¼ cup ketchup
¾ cup tomato paste
½ cup brown sugar, packed
½ cup molasses
½ cup apple cider vinegar
1 cup Buffalo Trace bourbon
(or your favourite kind)
Salt and freshly ground black pepper

MAKES **4** *cups*

Bourbon BBQ Sauce

IN A LARGE POT on medium heat, warm the oil. Add onions and garlic and sauté for 3 minutes, until fragrant. Add chili power, cumin, and cayenne and cook for 2 more minutes. Add beef stock, ketchup, tomato paste, brown sugar, molasses, and cider vinegar. Cook for 15 minutes. Add bourbon and cook for another 20 minutes. This will cook off the alcohol. When sauce is done cooking and cool enough to work with, blend using a hand blender or food processor. Add salt and pepper to taste. Let the sauce fully cool before bottling. It should keep for about 1 month in the fridge.

XIX Nineteen

ANDREW FUNG
▪ *chef* ▪

You've always had to drive a bit to get a taste of Andrew Fung's refined East-meets-West cuisine. First at Blackhawk Golf Course— where, as executive chef, Fung transformed its dreary clubhouse menu into dishes worthy of Jaime Oliver— and now as co-owner of two XIX outposts, both beacons of taste in suburbia's food deserts.

At the Terwillegar location, the expansive, elegant room has a seat for whatever mood you're in: kitchen booths (to see all the action), curved booths (for cozy dinners), white-linened tables (for business dinners), or the bar, where you might spot a hockey player or two. Look around: chances are good that every table is

sporting Fung's signature Tuna Twists—seared Ahi tuna and cilantro aioli on sweet-spicy Thai egg noodles spun neatly around a fork for a bold, civilized bite.

At the St. Albert location, the same menu shines, with a few bonuses: excellent service, superb Edmonton art, and spicy sambal oelek–kissed confit duck wings so good, it's impossible to eat just one.

Born in Hong Kong and trained in Vancouver, Andrew has a strong work ethic and a gracious demeanour. His seafood-forward menu is a hybrid of vibrant southeast Asian flavours and French and Italian classicism. The techniques that turn out his refined plates were mastered in Europe under Michelin-starred chefs—a big reason his sauces are consistently pitch-perfect.

"I'm an immigrant," he says, "and what makes Canada great is its multiculturalism. This menu is my version of Canadian cuisine." On his menu, citrus-soy-glazed pork belly steamed buns, beef short rib sliders, and crispy halibut with French curry cream sauce (the first sauce he learned to make) are all plated with delicate artistry and assembled from the country's best bounty: duck from Quebec; lobster from PEI; fish from Vancouver; and pork, eggs, beef, and organic vegetables from nearby farms.

Now that's worth the drive.

ASIAN SLAW

½ cup shredded carrots

¼ cup thinly sliced red cabbage

2 cups thinly sliced green cabbage

3 Tbsp brown sugar, packed

3 Tbsp apple cider vinegar

1 Tbsp water

1 Tbsp grated fresh ginger

¼ tsp salt

MONGOLIAN DRESSING

2 Tbsp soy sauce

2 Tbsp dark brown sugar, packed

1 ½ tsp fresh lime juice

¾ tsp vegetable oil

¾ tsp minced garlic

½ tsp grated fresh ginger

⅛ tsp sambal oelek (a garlic chili sauce)

Ingredients continued overleaf

SERVES **4** *as an appetizer*

Ahi Tuna Twists

Andrew's signature appetizer is a brilliant study in balance: hot noodles contrast the cold slaw, cooked offsets raw, creamy counters crunchy, sweet-sour evens out salty-spicy. This balance of contrasts is the secret to these delicious bites. That's why each component is critical, but, luckily, much of it can be made ahead of time. The aioli recipe makes more than you will need for this appetizer. Leftovers can be stored in a sealed container in the fridge for up to 2 weeks. Use it to enhance sandwiches, as a crudité dip, or in any way you would use mayonnaise.

ASIAN SLAW In a large stainless steel bowl, mix carrots, red cabbage, and green cabbage. Set aside.

In a saucepan on medium-high heat, combine brown sugar, vinegar, water, ginger, and salt. Heat until mixture is just boiling. Pour hot dressing onto the cabbage mixture and toss to coat. Cover the bowl and chill until ready to serve.

MONGOLIAN DRESSING Mix all ingredients in a small bowl and chill until ready to use. This dressing keeps well in a lidded jar for up to 1 week in the fridge.

Recipe continued overleaf

CILANTRO AIOLI
3 cloves garlic, minced
1 egg
1 Tbsp fresh lemon juice
1 Tbsp chopped cilantro
½ tsp salt
⅛ tsp freshly ground
black pepper
½ cup extra-virgin olive oil

TUNA
2 oz Ahi tuna
Salt and freshly ground
black pepper
1 Tbsp vegetable oil

ASSEMBLY
5 oz cooked Chinese
egg noodles
(Wing's brand preferred)
Cilantro, finely chopped,
for garnish

CILANTRO AIOLI In a food processor, combine garlic, egg, lemon juice, cilantro, salt, and pepper and purée until smooth and thick. Add olive oil in a slow stream and continue to process until mixture has formed a thick emulsion. Adjust seasoning with salt, pepper, and lemon juice to taste. Cover and refrigerate until ready to use.

TUNA Season tuna with a pinch of salt and pepper. Heat oil in a small frying pan on high, and sear tuna on all sides very quickly, about 3 seconds per side. You don't want to cook the tuna too much; it should still be raw in the middle. Remove tuna from the heat and allow it to rest.

TO ASSEMBLE In a small frying pan on medium heat, sauté egg noodles with Mongolian dressing until noodles are coated and caramelized. Do this step when you're ready to serve, because the noodles need to be served hot.

Slice tuna into 4 rectangular pieces, ¼ inch each.

Lay Asian slaw on the bottom of each of 4 plates. Using 4 appetizer-sized forks, twist hot, caramelized noodles into bite-size portions. Lay forks on top of slaw. Place 1 piece of tuna on top of the noodles on each fork. Dab with cilantro aioli, sprinkle with cilantro, and serve immediately.

1 halibut fillet (1 ½ lbs), skinless
3 **Tbsp** butter, divided
1 **lb** dry spaghettini
10 **oz** green beans
1 **Tbsp** grainy mustard

2 shallots, finely chopped
½ red onion, chopped
4 **cloves** garlic, minced
½ **cup** diced Roma tomatoes
4 basil leaves, finely sliced into ribbons

½ **tsp** curry powder
2 **cups** whipping (35%) cream
4 **tsp** Dijon mustard
Salt and freshly ground black pepper
Microgreens, for garnish

SERVES 4

Dijon-crusted Halibut
with Curried Vegetable Spaghettini

PREHEAT the oven to 450°F.

Bring two pots of water to a boil on high heat. Add salt to the first pot for your spaghettini.

Slice halibut into 4 portions, about 6 oz each (or have your fishmonger do it ahead of time). In an ovenproof pan on high heat, melt 2 Tbsp of the butter. Once the pan is hot, add halibut and fry until one side is golden brown, about 3 minutes (no need to flip). Transfer fish to the oven and cook for 5 minutes.

Meanwhile, cook spaghettini in boiling salted water according to package instructions.

Fill a large bowl with ice water and set aside. Boil green beans in your second, unsalted pot of water for 2 to 3 minutes or until a fork can easily pierce them. Quickly transfer beans to the ice water to stop them from cooking and to set the bright green colour. Drain and set aside.

Once halibut is out of the oven, allow it to rest for 1 minute. Then spread grainy mustard on top and set aside to rest. If you are concerned about the fish cooling down too much, turn off the oven and place fish in the oven to warm through for 2 minutes just before serving.

In a frying pan on medium heat, melt the remaining 1 Tbsp butter. Add shallots and onions and cook until translucent. Add garlic, tomatoes, basil, curry powder, cream, and regular Dijon mustard. Season with salt and pepper to taste. Cook until cream has thickened into a sauce consistency, about 3 minutes. Reserve about ¼ cup sauce for use in plating, then add cooked spaghettini to sauce and toss gently to coat.

To serve, use tongs to pile spaghettini in the centre of each of 4 plates. Add a layer of green beans, and top with a portion of fish. Pour 1 Tbsp of reserved sauce on top of each piece of fish. Finish with microgreens.

NongBu

JOHN AHN
▪ *chef & owner* ▪

What is Korean food? It depends who you ask, of course. Regional Korean cuisine varies wildly, and for John Ahn it is all inspiring, with perhaps one exception: the "melt cheese on it" modern trend. (He's not a fan.)

When John set out to open a Korean restaurant in Edmonton, he wanted to honour those varying tastes. He also wanted to share the simple farm-driven staples he'd grown up with in his parents' Korean-Canadian home in rural Alberta. John recalls long days, working until 10 p.m. before the family would finally come together to make and eat *pa-jeon* (savoury Korean pancakes). Nothing he found

in his research trip to Korea could quite match his taste-memory of those crisp pancakes, bursting with seafood and fresh vegetables. What choice did he have but to make his own?

With the help of three cooks, all from different regions of Korea, John set to work. The goal? To offer only the food they all thought tasted best. The result is a focused menu of simple, fresh dishes that feels almost like a thing of the past. But while the food is old school, the wood and steel decor with hints of Korean pop culture place NongBu in the here and now. The small plates are perfect with a glass of soju, or plum liqueur.

(If you have a few minutes, John will tell you all about it.)

Although NongBu has only been open since spring 2015, it's already obvious that this team is passionate, energetic, welcoming, and committed. We can't wait to see what they do next.

PA-JEON DIPPING SAUCE

2 Tbsp soy sauce
1 Tbsp rice wine
(cheongju — or substitute sake)
1 Tbsp white vinegar
½ tsp minced fresh ginger
Korean chili powder (gochugaru),
coarse grind, to taste (optional)
Sesame seeds, to taste (optional)

CUCUMBER KIMCHI (OI-SOBAKI)

1 cucumber, unpeeled,
cut into 3-inch sticks
1 Tbsp sea salt
1 cup water
½ bunch Asian chives,
cut into 2-inch pieces
½ medium onion, diced
1 medium carrot, julienned

1 Tbsp fish sauce
1 Tbsp Korean chili powder
(gochugaru), coarse grind
1 tsp minced garlic
¾ tsp finely minced fresh ginger
1 tsp granulated sugar
1 Tbsp sesame seeds

MAKES `3-4` *pancakes*

Seafood Pa-Jeon
with Dipping Sauce and Cucumber Kimchi

This recipe calls for a couple of less common ingredients: gochugaru and Asian chives. Asian chives are milder than regular chives and are sold under many different names (Asian chives, Chinese chives, nira, garlic chives, buchu, or jungguji). Try to find them, but you can substitute regular chives or green onions if you wish. Gochugaru is a kind of red pepper flake that has slightly less heat than regular chili flakes and adds a bright, fruity flavour. Stock it in your pantry and use it anytime a recipe calls for chili flakes or cayenne. In Edmonton you can find it at the Silk Road Spice Merchant.

PA-JEON DIPPING SAUCE In a small bowl, mix soy sauce, rice wine, vinegar, and ginger. Add chili powder and sesame seeds (if using) before serving.

CUCUMBER KIMCHI (OI-SOBAKI) Place cucumber sticks in a large bowl.

In a separate bowl, dissolve sea salt in water. Pour over cucumber. Allow to sit for 20 minutes, then rinse cucumber in cold water and pat dry with a paper towel. Set aside.

In a separate bowl, combine chives, onions, carrots, fish sauce, chili powder, garlic, ginger, and sugar. Allow to sit for 10 minutes.

Add fish sauce mixture to cucumbers and gently mix until all cucumber pieces are covered in sauce. Cover and place in the fridge and serve within 1 to 2 hours of adding the sauce. This dish will keep in the fridge for a couple of days, but the cucumber will become soft, so the fresher, the better.

To serve, stir the cucumbers one more time, then remove from the liquid using a slotted spoon. Place onto a plate and sprinkle with sesame seeds.

SEAFOOD PA-JEON

½ cup all-purpose flour
½ tsp salt
½ tsp rice flour
½ tsp potato starch
¼ tsp baking powder
½ cup cold water
2 Tbsp vegetable oil
6 green onions,
cut into 2-inch pieces
1 medium carrot,
julienned or finely chopped
9 large shrimp, diced
½ whole squid, diced

SEAFOOD PA-JEON In a large bowl, mix flour, salt, rice flour, potato starch, and baking powder. Add water and mix until you have a smooth batter. (You should get a thick, yogurt-like consistency.) Pour batter through a strainer to remove any chunks. Cover with plastic wrap and leave it in the fridge for up to 1 hour before using.

Heat oil in a medium frying pan (about 6 or 8 inches in diameter) on medium. While oil is heating, remove batter from the fridge and add green onions, carrots, shrimp, and squid to mixture. Stir gently.

Once oil is hot (it should shimmer and flow around the pan easily), cover the bottom of the pan with a thick layer of pa-jeon mixture and cook for 2 to 3 minutes. Flip pa-jeon over using a wide spatula. Use the spatula to press pa-jeon flat against the pan (this will help to get both sides golden brown), and cook for another 2 to 3 minutes. Once pa-jeon is golden and crispy, slide it onto a plate and serve immediately with dipping sauce and cucumber kimchi.

2 ¼ cup + 1 Tbsp water, divided

2 ½ tsp soy sauce

5 Tbsp granulated sugar

6 Tbsp white vinegar

2 tsp strawberry jam

3 Tbsp crushed pineapple

¼ medium onion, diced

½ tsp grated fresh ginger

½ tsp salt

2 Tbsp potato starch

3 cups all-purpose flour

1 tsp potato starch

½ tsp granulated sugar

½ tsp salt

3 ¼ cups water

1 medium egg

3–4 Tbsp vegetable oil, divided

MAKES **6** *rolls*

Gemma Roll

John's mother, Gemma, invented these crisp, savoury, and comforting rolls when John was a child. They are similar to a large spring roll, made with an eggroll stuffed with beef and vegetables, wrapped, and drizzled with a sweet-salty sauce. Although non-traditional, they hold a cherished place on John's menu and hopefully in your home, too.

GEMMA ROLL SAUCE In a small saucepan on medium heat, combine 2 ¼ cups of the water, soy sauce, sugar, vinegar, strawberry jam, pineapple, onions, ginger, and salt and bring to a boil. Reduce heat to low and allow it to simmer for 15 minutes.

In a small bowl, mix potato starch in the remaining 1 Tbsp water. Add to the pan and stir until sauce thickens. Keep warm on very low heat until rolls are ready to serve.

WRAP BATTER In a large bowl, mix flour, potato starch, sugar, and salt. Add water and egg and mix until smooth. Pour batter through a strainer to remove any lumps. You should have about 4 cups of batter. Pour the batter into a pitcher or large measuring cup, if you have one — this will make it easier to pour into the pan.

Warm a 12-inch frying pan on medium-high heat and cover the bottom with ½ Tbsp vegetable oil. Take the pan off the heat, pour ⅔ cup of the batter into the pan, and quickly swirl it to coat the entire bottom of the pan. Remove any excess batter (it will make the wrap too thick) and put the pan back on the heat. Allow the wrap to cook for 2–3 minutes until it looks dry all over before gently flipping and cooking the other side for 2 minutes until the wrap has light brown bubbles all over it.

Repeat the cooking process until you are out of batter. (Save a small amount for use in assembly.) You should end up with 6 wraps.

FILLING

2 Tbsp vegetable oil
12 oz medium ground beef
1 cup shredded cabbage
1 cup shredded carrots
1 cup bean sprouts
4 green onions,
cut into 1-inch pieces
Salt

ASSEMBLY

3 Tbsp vegetable oil
Sesame seeds, toasted,
for garnish
Chives, chopped,
for garnish

FILLING Heat oil in a medium frying pan on high. Add ground beef and cook until meat is about half-done (still pink in the middle).

To the same pan, add cabbage and carrots and cook for 1 minute, stirring occasionally. Add bean sprouts and green onions and cook until beef is no longer pink. Add a pinch of salt. Adjust seasoning to taste.

Remove the pan from the heat and pour off any excess liquid. Allow the mixture to cool in a strainer over a bowl until all excess liquid has drained off.

TO ASSEMBLE Place a wrap on a dry cutting board. Cover a third of the wrap with ¾ cup to almost 1 cup of filling, leaving about 2 inches of space around the edges. Fold over ends and roll wrap like a burrito, making sure it's as tight as possible. If there are any tears, drip a little excess batter into the holes to repair them. (They will cook up when you fry the rolls.)

If you have real trouble making the rolls or if the wraps tear too much (they do take a little practice), you can just fold it over like an omelette and fry it in the pan, flipping once. It's less elegant, but it works.

Repeat with the rest of the rolls and allow them to rest for about 15 minutes with the seam side down.

Heat oil in a frying pan on medium. Gently place 1 or 2 rolls into the pan (depending on the size of your pan). Use a spatula to carefully roll them around in the oil until the entire roll is golden brown, about 5 minutes.

Transfer rolls from the pan onto a paper towel to drain excess oil.

Once cooled slightly, slice each roll diagonally in half. Pile pieces in the centre of a plate and drizzle with sauce. Sprinkle with toasted sesame seeds and chives and serve immediately.

North 53

KEVIN CAM
· *owner* ·

Inside his sleek, luminous room with its sultry glow and chic regulars, North 53 owner Kevin Cam (front row, left) has created a wondrous place that is at once a dining destination and a neighbourhood haunt for 124 Street regulars. Bar and kitchen have no sibling rivalry here: it's equal parts lively cocktail bar and food-focused restaurant, all under a dramatic ceiling inspired by Givenchy designer Riccardo Tisci.

Tenders of the North 53 bar have created the city's best cocktails, one perfectly balanced, palate-thrilling drink after another. Top of that list is cocktail impresario Elizabeth Yu's (pictured back row, centre) spectacular Rosey Cheeks—

a dazzling Japanese unfiltered sake and saffron-rose-cardamom concoction inspired by the Persian ice cream of her (and my) youth. Be warned: one will not be enough. The Smoke + Oak Fashioned is another smash hit. Made with oaken gin and smoked maple syrup, it arrives in a smoked-filled glass with its own blue spruce coaster, blow-torched seconds earlier to create said smoke — an outlandishly enjoyable, hipsterly touch.

Aside from elevating Edmonton's cocktail game, North 53 has also added to the city's late-dining culture, which until recently was limited to greasy diners or, worse, the drive-through window.

This young crew of madly talented food nerds feeds night-owl tendencies with savoury griddled mushrooms and poached egg yolk, Filipino-style pork buns, and bewitching buttermilk fried chicken, brined with jalapeños for maximum juiciness inside, served until 2 a.m. on weekends. And early birds needn't despair: the dinner menu is equally stacked with chefy riffs on comfort food, served on mismatched vintage plates.

It's just the beginning for North 53. Come taste their world. — **TF**

SAFFRON ROSE SYRUP

2 cups water

2 cups granulated sugar

10 pods green cardamom, crushed

8 threads saffron

½ cup dried edible rose petals

ASSEMBLY

2 oz nigori sake

1 oz saffron rose syrup

¾ oz fresh lemon juice

1 egg white

Dried edible rose petals, for garnish

SERVES **1**

Rosey Cheeks Cocktail

Elizabeth Yu's Rosey Cheeks is a riff on Persian saffron, pistachio, and rose ice cream called **bastani akbar mashti**. *For a play on the classic saffron-and-rice combination, she combines golden rose syrup with* **nigori sake**, *an unfiltered, cloudy Japanese rice wine that is rich and slightly nutty from leftover rice sediment. Shaken to a gentle froth with an egg white and some fresh lemon juice, this cocktail is beautiful, delicate, and balanced. You'll have more syrup than you need for one cocktail. That clearly means inviting friends over and spreading the saffron-rose-infused love.*

SAFFRON ROSE SYRUP In a small pot on medium heat, combine water and sugar and cook until sugar dissolves. Remove from the heat and add cardamom, saffron, and rose petals. Allow to cool and steep for 12 hours in the fridge. (It will keep for up to 1 month.) Strain before adding to the cocktail.

TO ASSEMBLE Shake all ingredients in a tin shaker (martini shaker) with no ice to aerate the egg white. When mixture is frothy, shake with ice to cool it down and dilute it. Strain it twice and pour into a coupe glass (an old-fashioned champagne saucer). Garnish with dried rose petals (available at the Silk Road Spice Merchant on Whyte Avenue).

2 bottles green Tabasco

2 chickens (1 ½ lbs each)
4 cups buttermilk
2 ripe jalapeño peppers,
thinly sliced
1 tsp piri piri chilies, crushed
(or fresh bird's-eye chilies)

4 Tbsp kosher salt
Lard or canola oil, for frying
2 ½ cups all-purpose flour
1 cup cornstarch
1 tsp sea salt

SERVES **4**

Buttermilk Fried Chicken

The dried Tabasco called for in this recipe can be replaced with cayenne or any hot pepper powder. But if time allows, give it a try — it's special!

DRIED TABASCO If you have a dehydrator, pour Tabasco sauce onto a dish or tray so that it is lying as flat as possible. Place in your dehydrator and set it to a constant 140°F. The Tabasco should stay in for about 18 hours to ensure it's adequately dried.

If you don't have a dehydrator, preheat your oven to its lowest setting. Pour Tabasco sauce onto an ovenproof tray or dish so that it is lying as flat as possible. Place the tray in the oven and leave overnight, or for as long as it takes to become a hard mass.

Once cool, chip dehydrated Tabasco off the tray and grind it in a mortar and pestle or coffee grinder until it becomes a fine powder.

FRIED CHICKEN On a clean cutting board or table top, place chickens back-side up. Use your thumb to find the spot where the leg bone attaches to the back bone. Push down on the bone with your thumbs to dislocate the bone (this will make your knife work easier).

Using a very sharp knife, slice the breasts and legs off the bird. Cut the wings off the breasts and keep them whole. Cut the breasts in half lengthwise. Split the leg where the drumstick meets the thigh. Reserve the chicken carcass for another use (like making stock).

In a bowl large enough to hold brine and chicken, combine buttermilk, jalapeños, chilies, and kosher salt. Whisk together and then add chicken. Make sure chicken is well coated, then cover the bowl and leave in the fridge overnight or for at least 12 hours.

Recipe continued overleaf

When ready to serve, preheat your deep fryer to 350°F or bring a heavy-bottomed pot (preferably cast-iron) half full of lard or canola oil to 350°F (measure temperature using a digital thermometer).

Preheat the oven to 350°F. Prepare a baking sheet with a rack on it.

In a large bowl, mix flour, cornstarch, and sea salt.

While the oil gets hot, take the pieces of chicken, still wet with brine, and add them to the bowl with the flour mixture. Toss well so that chicken is completely dredged in the mixture. Allow chicken to rest in the coating for 10 minutes to make sure it is adhered and you have a nice, thick crust to turn golden brown.

When the oil is hot, remove chicken from flour mixture a few pieces at a time, giving it a gentle shake to get rid of any excess. Fry the chicken in batches of 3 to 4 pieces. When chicken is a deep golden brown all over, remove from the oil with a slotted spoon and place on the rack on your baking sheet. Bake in the oven for 7 to 8 minutes. Continue frying chicken in batches until done.

TO ASSEMBLE When fully cooked, sprinkle fried chicken evenly with salt and Tabasco powder.

Padmanadi

KASIM KASIM
· owner ·

Vegan *is not the curse word* it once was in Edmonton. But even as restaurants that cater to vegetable lovers have proliferated, Padmanadi manages to stand apart. It's the kind of place that can convert your father-in-law, who once called vegetarian meat substitutes "pointless," the kind of place that brings peace to a family who can't agree on where to eat, and where arguments are forgotten over steaming bowls of fragrant, hearty "chicken" curries, spicy green beans, and the flakiest paratha.

Owned and operated by the Kasim family since 2002, Padmanadi's cuisine blends their native Indonesian cuisine with Chinese, Thai, and Indian flavours. Strongly influenced by Buddhist temple cuisine, which doesn't use onion or garlic, Padmanadi's dishes derive their spectacular flavour from peanuts, chilies, turmeric, coconut, and other seasoning under-dogs of the kitchen.

Oh, and did we mention that they give generously to local charities and hold frequent fundraisers? Still not convinced?

Here's a secret: even if the food weren't delicious (and it is), locals would keep coming back just to see Kasim's smile. Or maybe in hope of being enshrined in one of the many customer photos that line the walls. Whether it's your first visit or your hundredth, it's impossible not to feel like you belong at Padmanadi.

2 bananas
1 can (14 oz) coconut milk
1 tsp ground cinnamon
1 tsp brown sugar, packed
1 tsp nutmeg
1 loaf sourdough white bread, sliced
(about 9 pieces)

½ cup vegan sour cream
¼ cup icing sugar
2 Tbsp fresh lemon juice
1 Tbsp margarine
Icing sugar, for dusting
Shredded coconut, toasted, for garnish
3 cups seasonal fruit

SERVES 3

Banana Coconut French Toast

Since Padmanadi is a vegan restaurant, they use margarine and vegan sour cream (easily bought in most grocery stores) in this recipe. Of course, you can substitute butter and regular sour cream if you choose.

IN A BOWL, gently mash bananas with a fork. Add coconut milk, cinnamon, brown sugar, and nutmeg, and whisk to combine.

Place slices of bread in a casserole dish. Pour the coconut-banana mixture overtop. If your dish is not large enough, soak in batches. Allow the bread to soak for 3 to 5 minutes.

In the meantime, whisk together sour cream, icing sugar, and lemon juice in a small bowl to create a vegan crème fraîche. Set aside.

Heat margarine in a large frying pan on medium. Add soaked bread slices to the pan (one or more, depending on the size of the pan) and cook for 1 to 2 minutes, until golden brown. Flip and cook the other side until golden. Repeat until you have grilled all your French toast.

Serve 3 slices of French toast per person with a healthy dollop of crème fraîche on the side. Dust with icing sugar and sprinkle with toasted coconut. Arrange fruit on the plate and serve.

1 **cup** egg substitute
(or 4 eggs)
⅓ **cup** cornstarch
¼ teaspoon salt
⅓ **cup** nutritional yeast

¼ **cup** dried oregano
1 ⅓ **cups** bread crumbs
Canola oil, for frying
1 **head** cauliflower, cut into florets
Salt

SERVES **4** *as an appetizer*

Cauliflower Fritters

SET OUT three medium bowls. In one bowl, whisk together egg substitute, cornstarch, and salt. This is your wet mix. In the second bowl, combine nutritional yeast and oregano. This is your dry mix. Place bread crumbs in the third bowl.

Fill a large, heavy-bottomed frying pan (preferably cast-iron) about halfway with canola oil and allow it to sit on medium heat for about 10 minutes.

Dip cauliflower florets in the wet mix, then coat in the dry mix, and finally coat with the bread crumbs. Set aside until ready to cook.

Working in batches of 10 to 12 pieces (or fewer — careful not to crowd the pan or cauliflower will steam rather than fry), fry the cauliflower in the oil until golden brown all over. Use a slotted spoon or spider to gently turn the cauliflower pieces to make sure they become evenly coloured. Transfer cauliflower fritters to paper towels to drain any excess oil.

Sprinkle with a bit of salt to taste and serve.

Tip: The chefs at Padmanadi add vegetable powders to the dry mix, but these are rarely commercially available. If you can find some, add some!

Red Ox Inn

SEAN O'CONNOR
chef

Most chefs (and restaurant critics) will agree that the mark of a great restaurant is consistency. And consistency is the defining characteristic of Red Ox Inn, Frank and Andrea Olson's tiny, 12-table gem, which for 20 years has delivered superlative meals and polished service in the Strathearn neighbourhood.

Andrea and Frank met at the restaurant in 1990; she was a waitress, he a beer sales rep. Five years later they married, bought the place, and built a restaurant that, 18 years on, continues to defy expectations: it's a fine-dining spot you'd expect to find downtown, but it's tucked away on a sleepy residential street. The minimalist

black-and-white room is modern, unusual for a strip-mall joint. And it's casual but also special and intimate—another reason for its staying power.

Executive chef Sean O'Connor's succinct menu of five starters, six entrees, and four desserts come in thoughtful portions that allow you to eat a civilized multi-course meal without feeling overly full or uncomfortably formal. Thanks to stints at Le Bernardin in New York (with celebrated chef Eric Ripert), Quay in Australia, and a year-long food exploration through Japan, China, and New Zealand, Sean's dishes are sophisticated, with assertive flavours.

Even ubiquitous chicken attains new heights in Sean's hands (consider confit of leg, served with duck-fat potatoes, mustard greens, and onion jam as a prime example). And he makes pork belly special with preserved zucchini, tomatoes, and leek soubise—a modern take on a decadent cream sauce invented by legendary 19th-century French chef Georges Auguste Escoffier. Invent a reason to cook it tonight.

PORK BELLY
1 Tbsp fennel seeds
1 Tbsp whole black peppercorns
1 Tbsp kosher salt
1 tsp pink curing salt
2 Tbsp granulated sugar
6 cups chicken stock

Pork Belly

with Zucchini Tomato Confit and Leek Soubise

This is a very special dish for a special dinner party. Make sure you give yourself a day or two to prep rather than trying to do it all in one day with guests arriving. Bonus: you're likely to have more vinaigrette than you need for this recipe. Bottle it and keep in the fridge for up to 2 weeks and use on other dishes, like roasted Brussels sprouts or grilled fish, or use as a dip for crudités.

PORK BELLY In a dry frying pan on medium-low heat, toast fennel seeds and black peppercorns until aromatic, 3 to 5 minutes. Using a spice grinder, small coffee grinder, or mortar and pestle, coarsely grind fennel seeds and black peppercorns. Combine kosher salt, curing salt, sugar, and ground spices in a bowl.

Tip: If you can't find curing salt, you can skip it, but without it the belly will turn an unappetizing grey.

Coat the meat of the pork belly with the salt mixture. Cover and allow the belly to cool in the fridge for 4 hours. Rinse the salt mixture off of the belly with cold water.

Preheat the oven to 220°F. Place belly, skin-side up, in a roasting pan large enough to let it lie flat. Add chicken stock and cover the pan with aluminum foil.

Cook belly in the oven for 8 hours or until soft. When done, leave belly in the braising liquid and place in the fridge overnight until firm. Remove belly from pan. Gently cut off and discard belly skin.

2 bulbs garlic

4 ½ cups + 2 Tbsp canola oil, divided

2 lemons, cut into 8 pieces each

2 Tbsp fresh rosemary leaves

3 Tbsp fresh thyme leaves

1 Tbsp whole black peppercorns

20 cherry tomatoes

4 large green zucchini,
cut into ½-inch pieces

Ingredients continued overleaf

Line a baking sheet with parchment paper. Place belly on the parchment, and layer another sheet of parchment on top, followed by a second baking sheet. Place a weight on the top baking sheet to press the belly. Leave it in the fridge for 4 hours. Cut the belly into portions about ½ inch to 2 ½ inches thick. You may end up with more than 10 portions (bonus!). Wrap any extra in plastic wrap and freeze in a freezer bag for later use.

ZUCCHINI AND TOMATO CONFIT Preheat the oven to 300°F.

Place each bulb of garlic on a piece of aluminum foil large enough to wrap around it. Pour 1 Tbsp of the canola oil over each bulb, then wrap with foil. Roast garlic for 2 hours or until soft. When cooled, peel cloves and discard skins. Set aside 1 bulb to use for soubise and vinaigrette.

In a large pot, combine the remaining 4 ½ cups canola oil, lemons, rosemary, thyme, peppercorns, and 1 bulb of roasted garlic.

Gently warm mixture over low heat and use a digital thermometer to maintain a temperature of 140°F for 1 hour. If you don't have a thermometer, you can just turn off the heat, cover, and leave it for 1 hour. Set mixture aside and allow to cool to room temperature.

Fill a large bowl with ice water and set aside. Bring a pot of water to a boil. Cut a small X shape in the top of each tomato, just through the skin and not the tomato itself. Boil the tomatoes for 30 seconds and then quickly transfer them into the bowl of ice water. (This process loosens the skins without cooking the tomatoes.) Gently peel the tomatoes and set them in the oil mixture.

In a grill pan (or frying pan) on medium heat, sauté zucchini until you see grill marks or the zucchini is just tender but not soft. Add to oil mixture. Refrigerate overnight, or for up to 3 days.

Recipe continued overleaf

SOUBISE

2 leeks, white and light green parts only, washed, and cut into ½-inch pieces
1 ½ Tbsp butter
¼ bulb roasted garlic
⅓ cup whipping (35%) cream
Kosher salt

VINAIGRETTE

4–5 salt-cured anchovies
¼ cup parsley
1 ⅔ cups extra-virgin olive oil
⅔ cup fresh lemon juice
¼ cup fresh rosemary leaves
¾ bulb roasted garlic
1 tsp Dijon mustard
Kosher salt

ASSEMBLY

2 Tbsp canola oil
Salt and freshly ground black pepper
Pea tendrils, for garnish
Watercress, for garnish

SOUBISE In a heavy-bottomed pot over low heat, combine leeks, butter, and garlic and gently cook until leeks are soft, about 10 minutes. Remove from the heat. Add cream and, using an immersion blender, purée until smooth. Alternatively, allow to cool and purée in a blender. Season to taste with salt.

VINAIGRETTE Rinse anchovies and pat them dry. Finely chop anchovies and parsley and set aside. In a food processor, pulse olive oil, lemon juice, rosemary, garlic, and mustard until you have a rough purée. Pour into a bowl and add anchovies and parsley. Season with kosher salt to taste.

TO ASSEMBLE Preheat the oven to 300°F.

Heat oil in a frying pan on medium-high. Sear pork belly portions until golden brown on all sides, about 3 minutes per side.

In a pot on medium heat, warm soubise.

Transfer 2 pieces of zucchini and 2 tomatoes per person onto paper towels to drain. Sprinkle salt and pepper over the vegetables and warm them in the oven.

To serve, place a spoonful of soubise on the bottom of each wide bowl or deep plate. Top with pork belly, zucchini, and tomatoes. Drizzle lightly with vinaigrette. Garnish with pea tendrils and watercress and serve immediately.

¼ cup pumpkin seeds, toasted
¼ cup walnut pieces, toasted
2 cups graham cracker crumbs
½ cup unsalted butter, melted
6 Tbsp granulated sugar
¼ tsp kosher salt

¾ cup whipping (35%) cream
4 sheets gelatin (gold)
4 cups cold water, for gelatin
⅔ cup granulated sugar
3 Tbsp water
4 egg yolks

1 ¾ cups cream cheese
3 Tbsp icing sugar
1 vanilla bean
1 ½ cups Greek yogurt

SERVES **10**

Whipped Cheesecake
with Pumpkin and Coconut

GRAHAM CRUST Preheat the oven to 350°F.

Roughly chop pumpkin seeds and walnuts. In a bowl, combine all ingredients. Gently pack into the base of an 8-inch square cake mould or 9-inch springform pan with a removable bottom (do not push up the sides). Bake for 20 minutes until the crust is golden around the edges. Allow to cool at room temperature.

CHEESECAKE In a bowl, whip cream to stiff peaks and set aside in the fridge.

Place gelatin sheets in a large bowl and cover them with cold water for about 5 minutes. When gelatin is soft, squeeze out excess water and set it aside for use later.

In a small pot on medium-high heat, combine sugar and the 3 Tbsp water and boil until it reaches 250°F (measured with a digital thermometer).

Tip: Don't use Knox gelatin here instead of the sheets — your cheesecake will be too stiff.

While syrup is cooking but has not yet reached 250°F, whip egg yolks with a whisk or electric mixer for 2 minutes, until their colour lightens. Once sugar mixture reaches 250°F, slowly pour syrup into the bowl with the egg yolks, mixing all the while with the whisk or electric mixer. Once all syrup has been poured in, whisk more vigorously until the mixture doubles in volume. Set aside.

In a heatproof bowl, combine cream cheese, icing sugar, and gelatin. Using a small knife with a sharp point, split vanilla bean in half, scrape out seeds, and add them to the bowl. Set over a pot of simmering water and gently stir to combine. When cheese and gelatin have melted, pour contents of the bowl into your egg yolk mixture. Place the bowl with the egg mixture and cream cheese mixture into a bowl of ice water, and whip mixture until it is cold and increases to about 1 ½ times its original volume. Gently fold in yogurt and whipped cream.

Pour cheesecake mixture into your cake pan on top of the crust and set in the fridge for 2 hours or overnight.

PUMPKIN CURD

4 eggs
6 egg yolks
1 cup pumpkin purée
½ cup unsalted butter
¼ cup granulated sugar
4 tsp brown sugar, packed
½ tsp ground cinnamon
¼ tsp nutmeg
¼ tsp ground ginger
⅛ tsp kosher salt

COCONUT WHIP

1 can (14 oz) coconut cream
½ cup whipping (35%) cream
3 Tbsp icing sugar

ASSEMBLY

½ cup pumpkin seeds, toasted
½ cup walnut pieces, toasted

PUMPKIN CURD In a heavy-bottomed pot over low heat, stir together all ingredients and heat until the mixture resembles a thick custard. Use a heatproof rubber spatula to stir your curd and prevent it from curdling or scorching.

Using an immersion blender, purée the mixture, then strain it through a fine-mesh strainer to get rid of any lumps or bits of overcooked egg. Allow it to cool in the fridge.

COCONUT WHIP Place unopened can of coconut cream upside down in the fridge overnight. Remove from the fridge, turn it right-side up, and remove the lid. The coconut water will be resting on top of the cream. Drain coconut water from cream and combine the coconut cream with whipping cream and icing sugar. Whip until stiff peaks form, 3 to 5 minutes. Keep refrigerated. (This recipe makes a bit more coconut whip than you'll need, but you can use it on other desserts or just enjoy it with a sprinkle of coconut and a spoon.)

TO ASSEMBLE Gently remove cheesecake from pan and cut into 8 or 10 slices. Spoon pumpkin curd on each plate and top with a slice of cheesecake. Dollop coconut whip on top and sprinkle with pumpkin seeds and walnuts.

Remedy

SOHAIL "ZEE" ZAIDI

• *owner* •

AJAY SINGH

• *chef* •

CHANDRA KANT

• *chef* •

The first time I ate at Remedy in the early 2000s, I was skeptical. My friends loved it, and everyone kept recommending it, but still, a coffee shop that sold Pakistani and Indian food? It just didn't quite make sense to me. Wow, was I wrong to doubt. One visit and I quickly became a fixture at the original location on 109 Street. Remedy's long-time owner, Zee (pictured centre), would laugh at me and encourage me to branch out from my standard order of a chana masala wrap. Ever since, my husband's go-to phrase when it comes to jolting me out of my stubborn ways is, "Leanne, it'll be like Remedy."

Remedy is a welcoming place, open late and inviting to those who want to linger over an ever-expanding list of homemade chais—the perfect·haunt for students and night owls. The students are easy to spot: desperate-eyed, huddled over computers, trying to savour their meal while finishing a paper or studying for an exam. Zee and chefs Ajay Singh and Chandra Kant (pictured right and left, respectively) have created a menu of items that comfort and satisfy in a uniquely Remedy way. Zee's experiences travelling, cooking, and even driving taxis in New York City shaped him into a person willing to take a chance on a new concept. Five locations later, Edmonton thanks him for trying—and I thank him every time I sink my teeth into a luscious, spicy pile of chickpeas.— **LB**

¼ **cup** canola or olive oil

1 red onion, chopped

2 **Tbsp** minced garlic

2 **Tbsp** minced fresh ginger

½ **cup** curry leaves

6 bay leaves

1 **tsp** ground turmeric

1 **tsp** ground cumin

1 **tsp** chili flakes

5 or 6 whole black peppercorns

½ **tsp** salt

6 **cans** (15 oz each) chickpeas

6–10 Thai chilies (optional)

¼ **cup** chopped cilantro, for garnish

Chana Masala

Most chana masala recipes involve cooked tomato sauce, but Remedy's iconic version skips it. The result is a spicy, bright flavour that is remarkably original. Learning to make this is like getting the keys to the secret palace. You won't believe something so delicious could possibly be so easy to make.

HEAT OIL in a large pot on medium. Add onion to the pan and let it cook until it starts to turn just a little brown, 5 to 10 minutes. Add garlic and ginger and stir. Let them cook until they also become golden brown, about 5 minutes. Add a splash of water to the pan if it seems like it is beginning to burn. This will deglaze the pan and make sure you still get all the lovely browned flavour. Add curry leaves, bay leaves, turmeric, cumin, chili flakes, peppercorns, and salt.

This is the masala part of the dish, and it's where all the flavour lives. Cook the masala, stirring occasionally, until it turns light yellow and the oil separates from the onions, 5 to 10 minutes.

Add chickpeas and the water from the cans to the pot and bring to a boil. Turn down the heat and simmer for about 15 minutes, stirring occasionally to keep masala from burning on the bottom of the pot.

Add Thai chilies (if using) and simmer for 5 minutes. Skip this step if you don't like your food spicy.

Serve chana masala in bowls, topped with cilantro, or, as Remedy does, wrapped in a pita for lunch on the go.

¼ **cup** canola or olive oil
1 red onion, chopped
2 Tbsp minced garlic
2 Tbsp minced fresh ginger
½ **cup** curry leaves

6 bay leaves
1 tsp ground turmeric
1 tsp ground cumin
1 tsp chili flakes
5 or 6 whole black peppercorns

½ **tsp** salt
1 cup diced potatoes
27 oz puréed or finely chopped frozen spinach (thawed)
1 cup paneer, diced

SERVES **6**

Palak Paneer

This creamy, green dish is a Punjabi specialty from northern India, made with creamed spinach (palak) and cubes of fresh cheese (paneer). Remedy's recipe calls for frozen spinach, but you can do half fresh or all fresh if you like. If you want it extra creamy, add a bit of Greek yogurt, sour cream, or a swirl of whipping cream. You can find frozen paneer in most supermarkets and Indian grocers. Skip the paneer if you want to keep the palak vegan.

HEAT OIL in a large pot on medium. Add onion and sauté until it starts to turn just a little brown, 5 to 10 minutes. Add garlic and ginger and stir. Let them cook until they also become golden brown, about 5 minutes.

Add curry leaves, bay leaves, turmeric, cumin, chili flakes, peppercorns, and salt. Cook, stirring occasionally, until it turns light yellow and the oil separates from the onions, 5 to 10 minutes.

Add diced potatoes to the pot. When potatoes get soft, about 10 minutes, add spinach (palak). Cook for another 15 minutes and add paneer. Cook until heated through.

Enjoy in hearty bowls with basmati rice or naan, or, if you're like us, both.

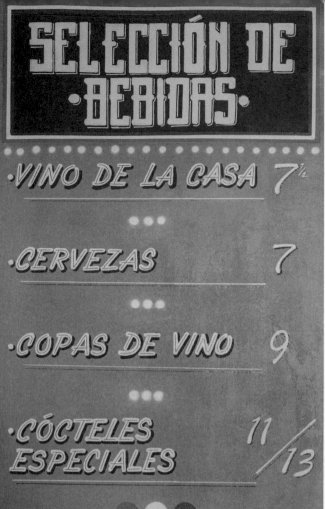

SELECCIÓN DE ·BEBIDAS·

·VINO DE LA CASA	7½
·CERVEZAS	7
·COPAS DE VINO	9
·CÓCTELES ESPECIALES	11 /13

Rostizado

CHRIS SILLS
· *owner* ·

DANI BRAUN
· *owner* ·

EDGAR GUTIERREZ
· *chef & co-owner* ·

You'd think opening the wildly successful Tres Carnales Taquería (page 210) would be a tough act to follow for owners Chris Sills, Edgar Gutierrez (pictured above), and Dani Braun, but the trio have one-upped themselves with Rostizado, where chef and co-owner Edgar serves up modern riffs on traditional Mexican *rosticerías* fare.

Up a few stairs in the historic Mercer Warehouse building is a boisterous room complete with loungey sofas, loud music, and retro TVs playing black-and-white Mexican films. The vibe is well-catered party, and resident social convener Chris keeps the good times

rolling as he roves around dispensing tequila and tales.

The well-catered part comes courtesy of standout starters like Ceviche de Robalo, made with lime juice, fresh Chilean sea bass, habanero chilies, orange, and avocado. It tastes as vibrant and lively as it looks. Move on to the main attraction: seasoned, slow-roasted Four Whistle Farm pork and juicy rotisserie chicken, served family style with potatoes that lazed below the roasting meats and soaked up their savoury drippings with every turn of the spit. Not a bad way for a spud to go. And it would be a crime not to leave

room for made-to-order churros — piping hot strips of fried dough rolled in cinnamon sugar with abandon. Don't forget the dulce de leche for dipping — so addictive, it ought to come with a warning label.

And of those aforementioned shots: tequila and mezcal (distilled agave spirit with a smoky edge) come by the ounce, or together as friends in crafty cocktails like La Bonita: made with fresh pineapple, cilantro and lime, and chili-infused mango nectar, it tastes like lying in an oceanside hammock. Party on!

1 **cup** granulated sugar
¼ **cup** water
8 **oz** cream cheese
2 **cups** evaporated milk
2 **cups** sweetened condensed milk
8 eggs
1 **Tbsp** vanilla
Sliced almonds, to garnish

SERVES **8-10**

Flan de Queso

This cream cheese flan is a luscious, quivery custard with a caramelly top similar to a French crème caramel. It is remarkably simple to make, but serve it to your guests and they will fawn without fail. It's an ideal dinner party dessert because it's made the night before and left in the fridge to chill and set. That leaves you free to focus on the mains the night of the party.

PREHEAT the oven to 300°F.

In a saucepan on medium heat, bring sugar and water to a boil. Cook until sugar turns golden brown, 6 to 8 minutes. This is your caramel. The longer you cook it, the darker it will become. The flavour will also deepen, with an enticing bittersweet edge.

While your sugar cooks, arrange 8 to 10 ramekins, each 4 oz, in a wide, ovenproof dish with high sides. Pour caramel into ramekins, dividing equally. You only need enough to coat the bottom of the ramekin, but a little more or less is fine.

In a blender, combine cream cheese, evaporated milk, condensed milk, eggs, and vanilla until smooth. Pour custard mixture through a strainer into a bowl.

Boil a kettle of water.

Evenly divide the custard among ramekins. Pour the boiling water into the casserole dish until it is halfway up the sides of the ramekins (a *bain marie*). Cover casserole dish with aluminum foil and carefully transfer it to the oven, making sure not to get the flans wet. The bain marie will ensure the custard cooks more gently and evenly to create that smooth, creamy texture.

Bake for 30 minutes. Remove flans and allow them to rest in the fridge for 24 hours to fully set and cool.

Flip flans out of their ramekins and serve caramel-side up, garnished with almonds, if desired. Expect some of the caramel syrup to puddle around the flan.

1–1 ¼ cups fresh lime juice

1 habanero chili, stemmed, seeded, and finely chopped

1 ¼ tsp kosher salt

5 mint leaves

¼ cup cilantro, with leaves and stems

1 lb sea bass, trimmed and cut into 1-inch slices

1 avocado, cored, peeled, and chopped

30 orange segments

Tostadas

SERVES **6** *as an appetizer*

Ceviche de Robalo

If you've never made ceviche because of the raw fish part, have no fear. This recipe is delicious, refreshing, and surprisingly simple. Marinating in lime juice denatures the protein, similar to cooking the fish, so all you have to do is keep this dish chilled until you're ready to serve. Use spanking-fresh fish and it'll make all the difference. To make larger amounts, simply multiply the marinade ingredients according to the weight of your sea bass.

IN A LARGE BOWL, combine lime juice, habanero chili, and salt. Mix thoroughly and gently.

Tie mint and cilantro up in a bundle with some string or cheesecloth and add to the lime juice marinade.

Add sea bass to the marinade and leave it to rest in the fridge for at least 2 hours before serving, or up to 24 hours, depending on how "cooked" you want the fish to be. You will know that the fish is ready to eat when it is opaque. Do not leave the fish for more than 2 days in the marinade.

Remove mint and cilantro bundle and serve ceviche with chopped avocado, orange segments, and tostadas.

Sabor

ADELINO OLIVEIRA
▪ *chef* ▪

Here's a sad fact: there aren't plenty of fish left in the sea. And that means that eating seafood in our landlocked province is fraught with ethical dilemmas—overfished oceans, harmful farming practices, and habitat damage, to list a few.

Lucky for us, there are no better advocates for sustainable fishing than Sabor co-owners and childhood friends Christian Mena and Adelino Oliveira. Sabor's western Mediterranean surf-and-turf menu is replete with every aquatic protein imaginable, all Ocean Wise certified. That means you can dine guilt free on Fresh Lobster Risotto, mussels in saffron cream,

octopus salad, and delectable squid and prawns on creamy white-bean purée, knowing it was all harvested sustainably.

While food is certainly the main event, Sabor is more than a restaurant to its co-owners—it's a creative outlet. Wednesday through Saturday, there's always live music, and Christian will sing a song or two. (In a past life, he was a lead in the Broadway hit musical *Rent* alongside Neil Patrick Harris.) And the menu is Adelino's canvas, a place where he can play with the food and flavours of his native Iberian Peninsula. (He owned three successful restaurants in Portugal.)

With Sabor's success, the duo decided to expand. Bodega, a splendid wine and tapas bar, is carved out from Sabor's front steps. With comfy bar seats and a charming patio, it's a favoured place for after-work drinks or people-watching along the boardwalk. Linger over sangria and small bowls of marinated olives and porcine nibbles—Portuguese chorizo flaming with grappa, or *pata negra*, 36-month-cured ham from the prized acorn-fed, black Iberian pig. A delightful way to spend a sublime but fleeting summer's eve.

1 lb russet or baking potatoes, peeled
1 egg
Salt and freshly ground black pepper
1 cup all-purpose flour

4 strips of bacon, cut into ½-inch horizontal strips
½ cup olive oil
½ large onion, diced
2 cloves garlic, minced

12 pearl or cipollini onions, whole
2 cups mixed mushrooms, chopped
1 cup red wine
1 cup chicken stock
Bay leaf

SERVES **4**

Pan-roasted Cornish Hen
with Potato Gnocchi Bourguignon

GNOCCHI In a large pot, cover potatoes in water and bring to a boil. Boil until tender enough that a fork pushes all the way through, 20 to 30 minutes. Drain potatoes, allow them to cool enough to work with, then mash until smooth. Add egg to the potatoes and season with a pinch of salt and pepper. Add flour a little at a time and stir with a wooden spoon until you have a smooth, sticky dough.

Turn out dough onto a floured surface and knead for about 3 minutes, or until soft and smooth. With floured hands, roll out small sausage-sized portions, then cut each sausage into ¾-inch pieces. Press each piece against the tines of a fork to form ridges.

Set aside in an air-tight container in the fridge for later use. (At this stage you can freeze them until you're ready to serve this dish. First, lay gnocchi in a single layer on a tray so that none are touching, and place the tray in the freezer for about 20 minutes. Once hardened, toss them into a freezer bag. Gnocchi can be frozen for up to 3 months.)

BOURGUIGNON In a medium pot on medium heat, cook bacon in olive oil until crispy. Add onions and cook until just golden, about 5 minutes, then add garlic, pearl onions, mushrooms, and red wine. Bring to a boil and cook until liquid is reduced by half, 10 to 15 minutes. Add chicken stock and bay leaf. Bring to a boil and reduce by half again, then remove from the heat.

CORNISH HEN

2 Tbsp butter
1 sprig fresh thyme
1 sprig fresh rosemary
2 Cornish game hens
(about ½ lb each)

Salt and freshly ground
black pepper
Microgreens, chopped parsley,
or baby arugula, for garnish

CORNISH HEN Preheat the oven to 500°F.

In a large ovenproof pan on medium-high heat, melt butter. Add thyme and rosemary.

To cut hen in half, insert the tip of sharp knife at neck cavity and firmly cut down along one side of the backbone toward the tail. You can also ask your butcher to do this for you, if you wish. Season hens with a pinch of salt and pepper and add to the pan. Sear the skin until golden and crispy, about 5 minutes per side. Flip hens over and sear until all parts of skin are golden. Transfer hens to the oven for 10 minutes, or until cooked through with an internal temperature of 165°F.

TO ASSEMBLE Bring bourguignon to a simmer and add gnocchi. Stir and simmer for 5 minutes. Discard bay leaf, then season with salt and pepper to taste.

Divide gnocchi bourguignon evenly among 4 deep plates or bowls. Top with half a Cornish game hen and a nest of microgreens, parsley, or baby arugula, and serve.

1 **cup** extra-virgin olive oil, divided
1 medium onion, sliced, divided
½ **tsp** ground cumin
Sea salt and freshly ground black pepper
1 **cup** white wine
2 **cups** white beans, drained
1 large potato, peeled and coarsely chopped

1 **cup** chicken stock
1 dry-cured Spanish-style chorizo sausage, sliced
2 **lbs** squid tubes, cleaned and sliced into rings
12 medium prawns, peeled and deveined
2–3 **sprigs** cilantro, chopped
½ fresh red chili, finely chopped (or ½ tsp chili flakes)
½ lemon

SERVES **4**

Squid and Prawns
with White Bean Purée

IN A SAUCEPAN on medium heat, warm ¾ cup of the olive oil. Add half the onions and cook until golden, 5 to 8 minutes. Add cumin, a pinch of salt and pepper, and white wine. Bring to a boil and cook until the liquid is reduced by half, 10 to 15 minutes. Add beans, potatoes, and chicken stock, and reduce heat to low. Cook until you can easily pierce the potatoes with a fork, 20 to 30 minutes. Remove the saucepan from the heat. Using an immersion blender, purée contents until smooth (you can also let the mixture cool and transfer it to a blender to purée). Set aside.

To a large sauté pan on medium-high heat, add the remaining ¼ cup olive oil and the chorizo. Warm for 1 minute, then add squid and prawns. Add remaining onions, cilantro, and chilies. Season to taste.

Cook until prawns are pink and cooked through, about 2 minutes. Turn off heat, squeeze lemon juice on top, and set aside. Reserve pan juices for serving.

In the centre of each serving dish, place a quarter of the bean purée. Top with a quarter of the cooked squid, chorizo, and onions, followed by 3 prawns. Drizzle with remaining pan juices and serve.

Shanghai 456

KAN WO WONG
- *chef* -

You don't come to Shanghai 456 for the scenery. In fact, you'd be hard-pressed to see a single pedestrian in this barren industrial strip in the northwest corner of the city. But those in the know make the trip anyway, on a quest not for breathtaking vistas but for chef Kan Wo Wong's faintly sweet and subtly spiced authentic Shanghainese food.

On any given day, the restaurant's 100 seats are packed with Kan Wo's devotees, munching on his all-made-from-scratch delights: sweet-savoury turnip and ham cakes, crispy duck, and the compulsively sapid spicy garlic eggplant, graced with a touch of

sugar and black vinegar, to name a few. And hardly anyone dines here without ordering a steamed basket of *xiao long bao,* Shanghai's renowned soup-filled dumplings. So popular are these physics-defying bites that Wong makes an astonishing 12,000 every month, each delicate, thin-skinned wrapper painstakingly hand-fluted into a round parcel, filled with savoury pork, and miraculously bursting with a soul-enriching broth.

Born in Shanghai, a port city near the mouth of the Yangtze River, Kan Wo learned how to cook at age 15. The Communist regime provided his housing, food, a $6 monthly stipend, and free training. The latter has served him well. He's won countless awards and owned restaurants in Taipei and Macau. He's cooked for dignitaries and royalty, and was a bit of star in Macau, where he hosted a weekly cooking show as head chef of Hotel Lisboa's celebrated 456 Shanghai restaurant, namesake of his Edmonton incarnation. Family life brought him to our fair city in 1996, and we've been dining out on our luck ever since. Who needs scenery when you've got food fit for an emperor?

4 dried shiitake mushrooms

1 tsp potato starch

½ cup + 2 tsp water (or chicken stock), divided

2 large long Chinese eggplants

2 ½ Tbsp vegetable oil, divided

1 tsp minced garlic

2-inch piece ginger, peeled and sliced into very thin strips

1 Tbsp sambal oelek (a garlic chili sauce)

1 ½ Tbsp granulated sugar

2 Tbsp light soy sauce

¼ tsp dark soy sauce (optional, for colour only)

½ cup thinly sliced or shredded pork

1 cup canned bamboo shoots, drained

2 green onions, cut into 1-inch pieces

2–3 Tbsp Chinkiang vinegar (Chinese black vinegar) or balsamic vinegar

SERVES **4**

Chinese Eggplant
with Spicy Garlic Sauce

HYDRATE dried shiitake mushrooms by soaking them in warm water for about 1 hour or until softened. Once hydrated, drain mushrooms, but reserve soaking liquid for another use. Rinse mushrooms under fresh water if there is any residual grit. Squeeze out the excess liquid from mushrooms with your hands. Trim and discard the tough stems, and slice the caps into thin strips and set aside.

In a small bowl, combine potato starch with 2 tsp of the water. Set aside.

Cut ends off eggplants and discard. Quarter eggplants lengthwise and cut into 3-inch pieces. Heat 1 Tbsp of the oil in a frying pan or wok on high. Add half of the eggplant and allow it to sear until brown on all sides, 3 to 5 minutes. Lower heat if it looks as if eggplant is starting to burn. You want to cook the eggplant until it starts to get soft and has nice colour. Remove eggplant from the pan and set aside on a plate. Heat another tablespoon of oil, and repeat with the remaining eggplant.

Make sure you have everything measured and ready because the next part goes very quickly. With your range hood fan running, heat remaining ½ Tbsp oil in a saucepan or in the same wok on medium, and add garlic and ginger and stir-fry for 30 seconds, just until fragrant, taking care not to burn garlic. Raise heat to high and add the chili sauce, sugar, and soy sauces. Cook for another 30 seconds. Add pork, hydrated mushrooms, bamboo shoots, and green onions and cook for another 30 seconds. Add eggplant and the remaining ½ cup water and stir. Cover with a lid and cook for about 2 minutes, until pork is no longer pink. Lift the lid and thicken with potato starch slurry if you wish (if it's thick enough, you may not need it). Add black vinegar, and stir-fry for 20 seconds. Adjust seasoning with soy sauce and vinegar. Serve immediately with steamed rice or noodles.

Tip: You can substitute fresh zucchini for the bamboo shoots, and you may omit the pork to make this dish vegetarian. Also, the mushroom's soaking liquid is packed with deep, rich umami flavour and slight smokiness, so don't waste it. You can use this golden liquor in the place of water or chicken stock in this recipe (it'll add a strong mushroom flavour), or freeze it and use it as the base of another sauce, a vegetarian mushroom gravy, mushroom risotto, or soup.

6 dried shiitake mushrooms
1 Tbsp potato starch
2 cups + 1 Tbsp water, divided
1 tsp sambal oelek (a garlic chili sauce)
1 Tbsp light soy sauce
¼ tsp dark soy sauce (optional)
½ tsp freshly ground white pepper

3 oz firm tofu, cut into matchsticks
3 oz pork shoulder or boneless loin cutlet, shredded or cut into ¼-inch slices
½ carrot, cut into matchsticks
1 Tbsp bamboo shoots (fresh or canned and drained), cut into matchsticks

1 egg
1 Tbsp Chinkiang vinegar (Chinese black vinegar or substitute balsamic or cider vinegar)
1 green onion, finely chopped, for garnish

SERVES **4**

Authentic Shanghainese Hot and Sour Soup

I first met Kan Wo and his business partner, Susie Chau, while interviewing them for a story on Chinese New Year food. Before I knew it, Kan Wo sent out a dozen dishes as if it were New Year's Eve, showcasing his mastery of the cold station and dim sum, as well as elegant entrees, hot pots, and desserts. The table was covered in plates, and during that interview he said Shanghainese food takes the best of northern and southern Chinese cuisine to create something distinctly its own. This soup is a perfect example of that, and the ideal companion on a cold, gloomy day.—**TF**

HYDRATE dried shiitake mushrooms by soaking them in warm water for about 1 hour or until softened. Once hydrated, drain mushrooms, but reserve soaking liquid for another use. Squeeze mushrooms with your hands to remove excess liquid, trim and discard tough stems, and slice caps into thin strips and set aside.

In a small bowl, mix potato starch and 1 Tbsp of the water and stir until completely dissolved. Set aside.

In a saucepan or wok, boil the remaining 2 cups water. Add chili garlic sauce, soy sauces, white pepper, tofu, pork, carrots, bamboo shoots, and mushrooms. Bring to a boil, then lower heat and allow it to simmer for 3 to 5 minutes, until pork is cooked.

Meanwhile, in a small bowl, beat egg and set aside.

Check soup and adjust seasoning with soy sauces to taste.

Use a spoon to remix your potato starch slurry, ensuring it is well combined. Using a ladle, stir soup from the centre in a steady circular motion, creating a whirlpool. Slowly pour slurry into the whirlpool in a thin stream. This prevents the starch from clumping. When you have added about three-quarters of the slurry, stop pouring and check consistency of the soup. It should be thick enough to coat your spoon or ladle. Add the rest if needed.

While soup simmers, use the same whirl-pooling technique to incorporate the egg. Make sure the motion is fast enough; otherwise, you will end up with egg clumps instead of the beautiful swirls or egg "flowers" (which is what Chinese people call them).

Add vinegar, top with green onions, and serve hot.

Tip: You can substitute some of the mushroom-soaking liquid for the water in this soup, if you'd like a strong, deep mushroom flavour.

Sofra

YUKSEL GULTEKIN

▪ *chef* ▪

Some foods are so much more than sustenance — they're symbols, emblematic of entire cultures and civilizations. Consider olives, or dates. Every time you take a bite, thousands of years of history burst in your mouth. That deserves celebration, and Sofra chef Yuksel Gultekin's menu does just that, offering up a joyous exaltation of the continent-straddling flavours of his native Turkey.

From nearly any seat in the house, you can watch the gregarious chef roll fresh pita dough (cooked to order) and place it in the open-flamed oven. Out comes thin, crispy-yet-soft, hot and buttery pitas for a trio of Sofra's

fabled dips—savoury-sweet date, creamy feta, and garlicky roasted red pepper—so perfectly matched, Fred and Ginger would applaud their harmony. Although delicious in their own right, the dips also help pass the time while succulent meats are being grilled for you, be it chicken, lamb, or spicy Adana kebab—ground beef laced with cumin and chili paste, and grilled on wide metal skewers for maximum smokiness.

For those in a nibble-and-sip mood, Yuksel and his wife and co-owner, Chandra Johner, opened an inviting wine bar downstairs. Mosaic lamps twinkle, and pillow-strewn seating on Turkish rugs set the scene for welcoming subterranean dining on a seasonal menu of shareable plates. Vine leaves stuffed with pine nuts and raisins, and feta-stuffed grilled apricots (Yuksel's mom's recipe) conjure the flavours of Istanbul's spice bazaars, where men play backgammon and bike couriers deliver trays of hot black tea in tulip-shaped cups. You can raise one of those cups here and nibble on a piece of honey-soaked baklava as your evening winds down—a sweet ending to a celebration centuries in the making.

2 marinated roasted red peppers
(available in most Mediterranean markets)
3 **cloves** garlic
1 **cup** thick, plain yogurt
(e.g., Balkan style)

3 **Tbsp** extra-virgin olive oil
1 **tsp** paprika
Salt and freshly ground black pepper
Pita, baguette, or French bread

SERVES **2**

Roasted Red Pepper Dip

THINLY SLICE red peppers lengthwise. Cut pepper lengths in half.
Crush pepper and garlic together with a mortar and pestle.

In a small bowl, combine the red pepper and garlic mixture with
yogurt. Add olive oil and paprika. Stir thoroughly. Season with
salt and pepper to taste.

Enjoy with pita, sliced baguette, or hand-torn chunks of French
bread or your favourite crusty bread. Can be enjoyed right away
or refrigerated for later. (It will keep for 3 to 5 days.)

HALIBUT

2 halibut steaks (6 oz each), skin on or off, according to your preference
4 Tbsp extra-virgin olive oil
½ tsp chili flakes
½ tsp cayenne
½ tsp salt

½ tsp freshly ground black pepper
Juice of 1 small lemon
8 slices beef pastrami (available at most Italian markets)
¼ small red pepper, finely sliced
½ small tomato, cut into 4 pieces

VEGETABLE SAUTÉ

1 ½ Tbsp extra-virgin olive oil
¾ small red pepper, diced
½ small tomato, peeled and diced
2–3 mushrooms of your choice, sliced
1 tsp dried oregano
Salt and freshly ground black pepper

SERVES **2**

Pastrami-wrapped Halibut

HALIBUT Pat halibut steaks dry. Cut each halibut steak in half width-wise and place in a dish with olive oil, chili flakes, cayenne, salt, pepper, and lemon juice.

Make sure halibut steaks are thoroughly rubbed with marinade and allow them to sit at least 4 hours (marinating 24 hours in advance will produce the best flavour and tenderness).

Preheat the oven to 350°F.

On a clean surface, lay 2 slices of pastrami (one on top of the other) and top with a few thin slices of red pepper.

Place one halibut portion on top of the red pepper and crown with a tomato wedge.

Repeat with the other pieces of halibut. Wrap pastrami around the halibut and vegetables. If you have trouble securing the pastrami, use a toothpick to pin it in place.

Place on a baking sheet and bake for 8 to 10 minutes.

VEGETABLE SAUTÉ Heat olive oil in a pan on medium. Add red pepper, tomato, mushrooms, and oregano. Stir well and add salt and pepper to taste.

Cook for about 3 minutes, stirring occasionally.

TO ASSEMBLE Place 2 wrapped halibut portions in the centre of each plate and top with vegetable sauté.

Solstice Seasonal Cuisine

JAN TRITTENBACH
· chef ·

JAMIN SHARP
· chef ·

Just when you thought you couldn't squeeze one more restaurant onto 124 Street, a quad of affable gents — executive chef Jan Trittenbach (pictured right), sous chef Jamin Sharp (pictured left), service and wine manager Jon Elson, and barman Joshua Meachem — quietly opened the 40-seat (plus 8 at the bar) Solstice.

The dark interior is a modest backdrop for Jan and Jamin's bright and modern seasonal fare, heavily influenced by Jan's Swiss background and Jamin's French culinary training and Italian and Spanish side trips. They shop the neighbourhood's 124 Street farmers' market, returning with ingredients for stellar dishes like

venison tenderloin with golden spätzle and sweet-tart blackberry gastrique, or the Pig's Tail—literally the tail of a pig, its meat cooked sous-vide, pulled, breaded, and deep-fried, served with legumes and bacon jam—so delicious, one customer has threatened to launch a petition to bring it back.

That's because, rain or shine, the entire menu changes with the seasons, and every three months it's as if a whole new restaurant appears. The four equal partners agreed the food, cocktails, brilliant off-the-radar pours, and even the art changes at every solstice and equinox, when the leaves turn colour or the days grow longer.

This attention to detail is the result of owner-operators who are truly both. On any given night, Jan or Jamin will cook your dinner, Jon will serve you and explain the wine list he created, and Joshua will mix a fine cocktail to start (or end) your meal. If it feels like you've stepped into their home, that's by design. An evening spent here comes with all the gracious hospitality you'd expect from a dinner with good friends—and that never goes out of season.

3 cups + 2 Tbsp all-purpose flour

2 tsp salt

White pepper

Pinch of nutmeg

6 eggs

½ cup milk

½ cup soda water

¼ cup chopped parsley

1 Tbsp canola oil

1 cup granulated sugar

2 cups white wine vinegar

2 cups blackberries

Pinch of salt and pepper

Venison tenderloin, trimmed of fat and silver skin (6 oz per person)

2 Tbsp canola oil

Salt and freshly ground black pepper

4 Tbsp butter, divided

1 red onion, diced

1 bunch Swiss chard, chopped

SERVES 2-4

Venison Tenderloin
with Spätzle, Swiss Chard, and Blackberry Gastrique

SPÄTZLE In a bowl, mix flour, salt, a pinch of white pepper, and nutmeg. Make a well in the centre of the flour mixture and add the eggs. Using a hand mixer, mix on low speed while slowly adding milk and soda water. Increase speed to medium and mix until a smooth dough forms. Let dough rest for 20 minutes.

Set a large pot of water to boil. Meanwhile, prepare a bowl of ice water. When ready to cook, press dough through a spätzle maker or a large-holed strainer or metal grater into a pot of boiling water. Cook for 5 to 8 minutes. Using a large slotted spoon, remove spätzle from the pot and place in ice water to stop the cooking. Drain well and toss lightly in oil to keep them from sticking together.

BLACKBERRY GASTRIQUE In a heavy-bottomed saucepan on medium-high heat, cook sugar, stirring frequently, until it dissolves and turns a light caramel colour, 3 to 5 minutes. Lower heat to medium and add vinegar. (Caution: sugar will create a dome and this might splash.) Let sugar dissolve again. Add blackberries and a pinch of salt and pepper. Let simmer for 5 minutes. Using a hand blender, blend until smooth, then strain through a fine-mesh strainer, reserving the

liquid. Return liquid to pot and keep warm until ready to serve.

VENISON Heat oven to 450°F. Place venison in a small ovenproof dish and bake for 3 to 7 minutes, depending on desired doneness. (Keep the oven on for assembling the dish.) Heat oil in a medium frying pan on high, then sear venison for about 30 seconds on each side. Season on both sides with salt and pepper.

TO ASSEMBLE In a hot, ovenproof pan on high heat, sauté spätzle in 2 Tbsp of the butter for 1 minute. Place in oven for 4 to 5 minutes, then flip and stir spätzle, and place in the oven to brown other sides. Remove from oven when done, but keep warm.

In a large frying pan on medium heat, melt the other 2 Tbsp butter. Add onions and sauté 2 to 3 minutes until translucent. Add Swiss chard and sauté until wilted, 2 to 3 minutes.

To serve, place 3 dots of gastrique around the outer edge of each plate and pile spätzle in the centre. Place wilted Swiss chard on top and crown with venison. Drizzle with remaining gastrique.

This recipe defies conventional wisdom of searing the meat first, then finishing it in the oven. In fact, it calls for the reverse. According to Jamin, this method cooks meat more evenly and the outside won't get overly dry or overcooked. Try it yourself and see!

BALSAMIC JELLY
5 sheets gelatin
2 cups cold water, for gelatin
½ cup white balsamic vinegar
8 Tbsp granulated sugar

BRIOCHE
4 ⅔ cups all-purpose flour, plus more, as needed, for kneading and dusting
¾ Tbsp instant yeast or ¾ oz fresh yeast
⅓ cup granulated sugar

2 Tbsp fine sea salt
7 eggs, divided
⅓ cup milk
1 ½ + 1 Tbsp unsalted butter, diced (½-inch cubes)

SERVES **10** *as appetizers*

Chicken Liver Pâté
with Balsamic Jelly on Brioche

If a glance down this multi-part recipe introduces any trepidation, fear not. It may look complicated, but since each component must be made the day before, you'll have little to do when it's time to serve. To make matters easier, you can buy the jelly or brioche. However you tackle it, this is an indulgent starter that will make an impression. Pair with Champagne for bonus points!

BALSAMIC JELLY Line a 3 × 4-inch dish with plastic wrap.

Bloom gelatin by placing sheets in a bowl with cold water for about 5 minutes.

In a small pot on medium, heat vinegar and sugar until sugar dissolves, then remove from the heat. Drain gelatin, squeezing out excess water, add it to heated vinegar, and mix well. Pour into the plastic wrap–lined dish to a depth of about an inch. Refrigerate until set, about 4 hours. (This jelly keeps well in the fridge for up to 2 weeks.)

BRIOCHE Place flour and yeast into bowl of a stand mixer fitted with a paddle attachment, and mix. Add sugar, salt, 6 of the eggs, and milk and mix on low until the mixture just forms a dough, about 2 minutes, then switch to a dough hook attachment and continue to mix for another 20 minutes. Now begin to add butter slowly, one cube at a time. Scrape sides of bowl twice when mixing in the butter. Add final butter cubes and mix for 10 minutes. When done, you will have a smooth, soft dough. If the dough is a bit too sticky to the touch, sprinkle about 1 Tbsp flour over the dough so that you can work with it more easily.

On a lightly floured surface, stretch, fold, and shape dough into a ball and place in a lightly oiled bowl in a warm spot for 1 hour. Repeat the stretch-fold-shape step and place it back into the bowl. Wrap the bowl tightly with plastic wrap and refrigerate overnight.

When ready to bake brioche, grease two 2 ½ × 5-inch loaf pans with butter, then dust with flour and shake the excess flour out, or spray pans with non-stick spray and line with parchment paper to prevent sticking.

Segment dough that has rested overnight into 2 oz portions and roll into 12 balls.

CHICKEN LIVER PÂTÉ

1 lb chicken livers
1 cup whole milk
2 bay leaves
1 clove garlic, minced

½ cup brandy
½ cup ruby port
1 ½ cups + **2 Tbsp** butter, cold, divided

2 Tbsp canola oil
1 shallot, minced
2 Tbsp capers, soaked in warm water for 5 minutes and drained

3 large sage leaves, finely chopped
3 Tbsp chicken stock (optional)

Set 6 balls in each pan, cover with plastic wrap, and proof for 3 hours. Proofing is the "second rising" of the dough, where the yeast does its work and the dough develops its volume and soft texture.

After the 3 hours are up, fill a cake pan or casserole dish with extra-hot tap water and place it on the bottom rack of a cold oven. Do not turn on your oven. Place the dough pans, still covered in plastic wrap, on the middle rack of your oven and close the oven door for about 90 minutes, or until dough has doubled in size. Don't open the oven door — humidity is important to this stage.

Once proofed, remove dough and water from the oven and preheat the oven to 350°F. Lightly beat remaining egg and brush the tops of the dough. Bake for 20 to 25 minutes, then remove from the pan and cool on a wire rack.

CHICKEN LIVER PÂTÉ Use a paring knife to trim the fat, membranes, and bile ducts from chicken livers, then rinse them. Pour milk into a small bowl, add livers, and cook overnight in the fridge to draw out impurities.

Drain the livers, rinse with water, and drain again, then pat dry with paper towel. Transfer the livers to a glass dish. Add bay leaves and garlic, then drizzle brandy and port over the livers. Toss briefly and gently. Cover loosely with plastic wrap and refrigerate at least 6 hours, or overnight.

Remove livers from the marinade and pat them dry with paper towels. Set a fine-mesh strainer over a small bowl and strain the marinade. Reserve the bay leaves and garlic separately.

Heat a heavy sauté pan on medium heat.

Add 2 Tbsp of the butter and oil and heat until the butter is foaming. Add shallots, capers, sage, and reserved bay leaves and garlic to the pan and sauté for 1 minute.

Season livers with a pinch of salt and arrange them in the pan in a single layer. Cook, using tongs or a large kitchen spoon to turn livers, until edges are brown but still pink inside, 4 to 5 minutes, taking care to not overcook.

Pour in reserved marinade and stock (if using) and raise heat to medium-high. The stock will add a bit more body and flavour to the pâté, so use it if you have it around. Cook, shaking the pan occasionally, until the marinade reduces slightly and begins to glaze the livers, about 5 minutes. Remove the pan from the heat and use tongs or a slotted spoon to remove bay leaves and discard. Allow liver and liquid to cool in the pan.

Transfer the contents of the pan to a food processor and pulse to a coarse purée. Add the remaining 1 ½ cups cold butter a few pieces at a time, pulsing after each addition to incorporate the butter and achieve a smooth consistency.

Fill a wide, deep bowl halfway with ice water. Using a rubber spatula, scrape the liver purée into a smaller stainless steel bowl and set it in the ice water. Whisk the purée until fluffy. The ice water will keep it cold and maintain the emulsification. Transfer to a serving bowl or refrigerate in an airtight container.

TO ASSEMBLE Cut the balsamic jelly into ½ × ¾-inch cubes and place on a platter with brioche buns and pâté. Serve with greens lightly dressed with oil and vinegar.

The Sugarbowl

ABEL SHIFERAW
▪ *owner* ▪

It's not overstating matters to call The Sugarbowl an Edmonton institution, much like The Closerie des Lilas was to 1920s Paris, where Hemingway wrote *Fiesta* and F. Scott Fitzgerald read aloud to him from *The Great Gatsby*.

Since 1943, The Sugarbowl has been attracting artists and university students. Its original brick walls serve as a backdrop for creatives who use the café as their office and academics who debate well past midnight over a pint from its list of 160 craft and Belgian brews. In fact, this bustling breakfast–coffee shop–bistro–pub opens at 8 a.m. and closes at 2 a.m., leaving just enough time for a scrub-down before it all begins again.

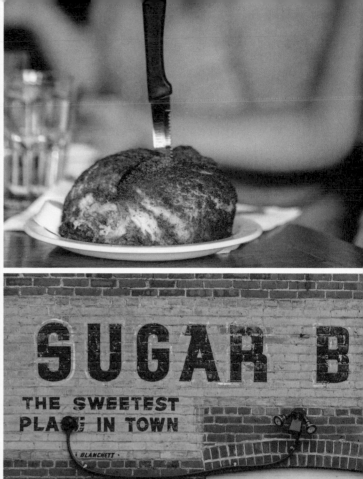

The early-morning crowd knows The Sugarbowl's sticky, sweet-scented cinnamon buns don't last long (they're gone by noon). Rest assured, these are not your overly frosted, gummy, mall-variety buns. These joy-inducing miracles are huge mounds of fluffy soft dough laced with the perfect amount of cinnamonny goodness. They're not too sweet, yet the crunchy brown sugar crust means you don't need (and it doesn't come with) any frosting.

For a satisfying meal, The Sugarbowl's free-run Lamb Burger, spiced with cumin, harissa, and rosemary, is undoubtedly one of the best burgers in the city. Topped with chèvre, caramelized onions, and rosemary aioli on a soft brioche bun, it's equally good while people-watching on the sun-drenched patio or in a cozy nook with a good book—and a cold beer, of course.

Given all of this, it's not hard to imagine that The Sugarbowl will be around for another 70 years. We'll raise a pint to that.

ROSEMARY LEMON AIOLI

1 cup mayonnaise

2 Tbsp chopped fresh rosemary

3 Tbsp lemon juice

1 ½ Tbsp lemon zest

3 cloves garlic

1 ½ tsp sea salt

2 tsp black pepper

CARAMELIZED ONIONS

2 Tbsp butter

1 large onion, cut into half moons

½ tsp salt

BURGERS

2 eggs

4 Tbsp fresh lemon juice

1 onion, finely chopped

4 cloves garlic, minced

½ cup finely chopped fresh mint leaves

½ cup finely chopped parsley

2 jalapeño peppers, stemmed, seeded, and finely diced

½ cup fresh rosemary leaves, finely chopped

½ Tbsp smoked paprika

½ Tbsp harissa paste

1 Tbsp dried oregano

1 Tbsp ground cumin

½ Tbsp ground allspice

2 ½ Tbsp salt

2 ½ Tbsp freshly ground black pepper

3 lbs lean ground free-range lamb

2 Tbsp olive oil

18 oz goat cheese

ASSEMBLY

6 brioche buns

2 tomatoes, sliced

12 lettuce leaves

SERVES **6**

Lamb Burger

ROSEMARY LEMON AIOLI Add all ingredients to a small bowl. Using a hand blender or food processor, blend until smooth. Cover and leave in in the fridge until you're ready to use it. It should keep for 3 to 4 weeks.

CARAMELIZED ONIONS In a large frying pan over low heat, melt butter. Add onions and salt and cook very slowly, for 20 to 30 minutes, stirring occasionally. If onions stick to the pan, add a bit of water to deglaze it. The sticky stuff is the delicious caramelization. Once onions are as darkly caramelized as you like, remove from the heat.

BURGERS In a very large bowl, whisk eggs and lemon juice. Add onions, garlic, mint, parsley, jalapeños, rosemary, paprika, harissa paste, oregano, cumin, allspice, salt, and pepper. Add ground lamb and mix until combined. Shape into 6 burger patties about 8 oz each. (You can make them smaller and have more burgers, if you like).

Heat olive oil in a large non-stick frying pan on medium. Add patties either one at a time or more, depending on the size of your pan. Fry for 4 minutes on one side, then flip and cook for another 3 minutes. Add about 3 oz of goat cheese to the top of each patty and cook for another 2 minutes, just to melt the cheese a bit. Adjust the cooking time based on your desired doneness.

TO ASSEMBLE While the burgers cook, toast the buns quickly on a grill or using your oven's broiler. Slather each bun with rosemary lemon aioli. Lay your burger patty on the bottom and top with caramelized onions, slices of tomato, and lettuce.

6 cups all-purpose flour
1 Tbsp instant yeast
⅔ cup granulated sugar
2 eggs
1 cup unsalted butter, room temperature

1 ¾–2 cups water
Canola or vegetable oil, for greasing
½ cup unsalted butter, melted, plus more for greasing
1 ½ cups dark brown demerara sugar, packed
2 Tbsp ground cinnamon

MAKES **6** *buns*

Cinnamon Buns

These buns are legendary — and huge! Soft, fluffy, and somewhere between sweet bread and pastry, brown sugar all crispy and caramelized, they take a little longer than your usual cinnamon buns, both in preparation and cooking time, but trust us — they are worth every second of it. You'll need to make the dough the night before you want to eat them.

IN A LARGE BOWL, combine flour, yeast, and sugar. Crack eggs into a small bowl and whisk.

Make a well in the centre of your flour mixture and drop in (approximately) tablespoon-sized pieces of butter until 1 cup of butter is added. Add eggs and 1 ¾ cups of water. In a large mixer with a dough hook, or using your hands, mix dough. Bring dough together roughly and then knead. The dough should be quite wet and sticky. If it seems too dry, add up to ¼ cup more water.

Knead for about 5 minutes, until dough is fairly smooth. It doesn't have to be perfect; the yeast will do a lot of the work for you. Lightly oil a bowl, and transfer dough to it. Cover the bowl with plastic wrap, and leave in the fridge overnight.

In the morning, remove dough from the fridge. Allow it to sit for about 1 hour and come to room temperature.

Grease a large baking dish or baking sheet with butter.

Melt ½ cup of butter on the stovetop or in the microwave. Mix brown sugar and cinnamon together in a large bowl.

Split dough into 6 pieces of about 12 oz each. Roll each piece of dough into a long log. Dip in melted butter, covering completely. Then dip butter-covered dough in sugar and cinnamon mixture. The dough will be soft, so it may stretch out into a longer snake. That is fine.

Tie the piece of dough into a knot, tucking extra pieces underneath. Dip the top of the knot into the cinnamon sugar mixture one more time and place bun in the buttered pan. Repeat until all 6 buns are made.

Turn the oven to 325°F and place buns on top of the oven to allow them to rise for 20 to 30 minutes.

Bake for 50 minutes. Insert a skewer into the centre of a bun to test doneness. If it comes out clean, the buns are done. If it is a bit wet, bake for 5 more minutes. Allow them to cool and enjoy.

Tres Carnales

CHRIS SILLS
▪ *owner* ▪

DANI BRAUN
▪ *owner* ▪

EDGAR GUTIERREZ
▪ *chef & co-owner* ▪

Sometimes a name says it all, and in the case of Tres Carnales Taquería (literally "the three homeboys taco shop" in Spanish), that's exactly what you'll get: the creativity of three great friends serving fantastic tacos.

Restaurant veterans Dani Braun and Chris Sills (centre and left, respectively) hashed out the idea of a taqueria serving Mexican street food over a bottle of Nicaraguan rum while vacationing in, you guessed it, Mexico. They recruited Red Seal chef Edgar Gutierrez (right) and, in 2011, opened a no-reservations, casual 40-seater so popular that local faithful still happily wait in lines that snake around the block.

From the moment you walk in, the street vibe grabs you: the bold graffiti (25 hours of freehand spray painting by Trevor Peters), the wall of homage to *Día de los Muertos* (Day of the Dead), and the unapologetically raucous music all hint at feisty flavours on the short but delicious menu.

Tacos de Pollo is a classic. Local, free-range chicken mingles with fiery chipotle peppers and salsa verde in soft, locally made corn tortillas. Al Pastor is another fine creation: marinated local pork slow-roasted on a spit, shaved and served with a fire-roasted pineapple-habanero salsa. It comes as a taco, torta (sandwich), or quesadilla.

You'll need napkins to maintain some propriety, but that's the joy of street food done right. The bold flavours here benefit from Gutierrez's refined instinct to balance fat with acid, hot with cold, soft with crunch. Dive into a messy fish taco and see why Tres Carnales Taquería lives up to its name.

6 tomatillos, husks removed
¼ white onion, diced
½ serrano chili
25 sprigs cilantro
1 Tbsp salt

1 can (7 oz) chipotles in adobo
1 white onion, chopped
½ bunch cilantro
¾ cup lime juice

3 cloves garlic
2 Tbsp canola oil
1 Tbsp salt
10 chicken thighs, skinless and preferably boneless

40 small corn tortillas
1 white onion, diced
Cilantro leaves, for garnish
3–4 limes, cut into wedges

MAKES **20** *tacos*

Tacos de Pollo

QUICK SALSA VERDE Place tomatillos, onions, and serrano chili in a pot and cover with water. Bring to a quick boil on high heat. Remove from the heat. Drain cooking water into a bowl and set aside for later use.

Combine cooked tomatillos, onions, serrano, and ½ cup of the reserved cooking liquid to a blender or food processor along with cilantro and salt. Blend until smooth. If it's too thick, add a bit more cooking liquid. Allow to cool to room temperature before serving.

Tip: This recipe makes more salsa verde than you need for these tacos. Store in a Mason jar in the fridge for up to 2 weeks. It's delicious on eggs, in grilled cheese sandwiches, and, of course, with Tres Carnales's Rajas con Crema Quesadillas (page 214).

TACOS DE POLLO Preheat the oven to 425°F.

In a blender or food processor, combine chipotles, onions, cilantro, lime juice, garlic, canola oil, and salt and blend until smooth. Set aside.

Arrange chicken thighs in a casserole dish large enough to fit them comfortably. Pour about ¼ cup of the chipotle mixture over each thigh. Cover the dish with aluminum foil and bake for 20 minutes (or until thighs reach 165°F). Allow the chicken to cool, then shred or chop and set aside.

TO ASSEMBLE In a dry pan, heat 2 soft corn tortillas layered on top of each other. Flip and warm until hot on both sides. Remove from the pan and place on a plate. Place a spoonful of chicken in the middle of the tortillas and top with diced onions and cilantro to your taste. Serve with fresh lime wedges and salsa verde.

Tip: If you have leftovers, add your favourite style of eggs to the chicken, salsa, and tortillas for a quick huevos rancheros.

2 cups poblano chilies
2 Tbsp canola oil, divided
1 white onion, sliced
2 cups corn kernels, fresh or frozen
2 cups crema (or sour cream)
2 Tbsp vinegar

1 Tbsp cornstarch
2 Tbsp salt
20 large corn tortillas
1 ½ cups queso blanco
(white Mexican cheese)
or mozzarella, grated

Rajas con Crema Quesadillas

PREHEAT the oven to 400°F. On a baking sheet, lay out poblano chilies. Lightly brush with about 1 Tbsp of the oil and roast until the skin is blistered and peeling off, 15 to 30 minutes; check and rotate so that both sides are charred. Place poblanos in a bowl, cover with plastic wrap, and allow them to steam for 10 to 15 minutes. This will make the skin easier to peel.

Using a paring knife, cut into each poblano and remove seeds. Lay pepper flat and scrape off the blistered skin, then cut into thin strips that match the size of your sliced onions.

Heat remaining 1 Tbsp canola oil in a pot on medium, and add onions. Cook until translucent, about 5 minutes. Add poblano strips, corn, and crema, and cook until just warm.

In a small bowl, mix vinegar with cornstarch until dissolved, then add to the pot along with salt. Bring the mixture to a boil while stirring frequently, about 5 minutes. This will keep your sauce thick and smooth. Taste and adjust seasonings. If you can still taste the cornstarch, cook a few more minutes.

In a dry pan, heat 1 soft corn tortilla. With the tortilla still in the pan, add about 1 Tbsp cheese and a spoonful of the poblano mixture on one half of the tortilla. Cook for 30 seconds, then fold the tortilla over to enclose the rajas. Cook until tortilla is crispy and cheese is melted. Serve with room-temperature salsa verde (page 213).

Tzin

COREY MCGUIRE
▪ *chef* ▪

Stroll past the Art Deco exterior of Tzin—a delightful wine and tapas bar so tiny you'd miss it if you blinked—and chances are you'll see chef Corey McGuire through its large window on 104 Street, prepping dinner and smiling back.

From a kitchen the size of an elevator, Corey puts out finely composed small plates with bold flavours, sourced from local growers and the Saturday farmers' market outside his steps. Case in point: his simply titled "Bacon" is a world of hedonic flavours consisting of crostini topped with homemade apple mayo,

Juicy Irvings Farm pork belly, and maple balsamic apple compote — all drizzled with calvados gastrique.

Inside, Kelsey Danyluk and her husband, Glenn Quinn, are your gracious hosts. The intimate bar — which, with only 20 seats, is more like their living room — is warm and eclectic, just like them.

Be adventurous and choose the menu's "feed me" option — by far one of the most fun ways to eat in the city. Simply tell Corey how much you want to spend, alert him to any allergies, and he'll send out a panoply of exquisite dishes from on and off the menu — say, spicy chorizo and shrimp paella or duck breast with orange paprika barbecue sauce — until you're full. While you're at it, add half-pours of wines, perfectly matched to each dish from Kelsey's thoughtful, well-priced list of Old World classics and Canadian winners.

BRAISED BACON

2 lbs (or more) whole slab bacon
4 cups chicken stock
2 cups apple juice
⅓ cup apple cider vinegar
1 bay leaf
2 tsp whole black peppercorns

COMPOTE

2 Pink Lady apples, diced
2 Tbsp brown sugar, packed
1 Tbsp fresh lemon juice
1 Tbsp canola oil
¼ red onion, diced
⅓ cup maple balsamic vinegar
Salt

SERVES **4**

Braised Bacon Crostini
with Calvados Gastrique

Bacon this good requires time — a few hours' braise and an overnight stay in the fridge — so start this the day before you want to serve it. In fact, the other elements (maple balsamic compote, apple mayo, and calvados gastrique) can be made the day before, too, so all you have to do is assemble these tasty nibbles and watch your guests inhale them.

BRAISED BACON Preheat the oven to 300°F.

Place all ingredients in a large ovenproof pot with a tight-fitting lid. Bring liquid to a boil and then transfer the pot to the oven with the lid on for 2 to 3 hours, or until the bacon is soft and very tender. Remove bacon from the liquid, cover it, and allow it to rest in the fridge overnight.

COMPOTE Combine apples, brown sugar, and lemon juice in a bowl and allow to sit for 1 hour.

In a large sauté pan on medium heat, warm canola oil. Add onions and sauté until just translucent, about 5 minutes. Add maple balsamic vinegar and bring to a simmer. Add apple mixture and cook until apples are warm.

Using a strainer or colander over a bowl, strain apples and onions and place them in a separate bowl. Return liquid to pan and bring to a simmer. Allow it to cook until it has reduced to a thick syrup, 15 to 20 minutes on a low simmer. Pour syrup over apples and onions and stir. Add salt to taste. Allow to cool to room temperature, then cover and store in the fridge.

Tip: Tzin sources its maple balsamic vinegar from Evoolution, its 104 Street neighbour. Corey says that maple flavour is integral to the dish. If you can't find maple balsamic in your area, you may use regular balsamic vinegar, but substitute maple syrup for the brown sugar to infuse some maple flavour.

MAYONNAISE

2 egg yolks
2 tsp apple cider vinegar
2 tsp grainy mustard
1 tsp salt
1 tsp granulated sugar
2 cups canola oil, divided
⅓ cup apple juice
Salt

GASTRIQUE

2 Tbsp water
½ cup granulated sugar
⅓ cup apple cider vinegar
5 tsp calvados (apple brandy)

ASSEMBLY

1 baguette, cut into ½-inch slices

MAYONNAISE In a food processor, combine egg yolks, vinegar, mustard, salt, and sugar. Mix until frothy and slightly thickened. With the processor running, slowly add 1 cup of the oil. Add the apple juice slowly, followed by the remaining 1 cup oil. Season to taste with salt and a little more cider vinegar. Cover and place in the fridge, where it will keep for only 10 to 14 days because of the raw egg yolk.

GASTRIQUE Put water in a large pot. Add sugar, taking care not to get any on the sides of the pot. Do not stir.

On high heat, bring sugar water to a boil until sugar turns golden. Working quickly and carefully, whisk in vinegar and calvados a bit at a time until incorporated. It will splatter and bubble, but just keep whisking. Allow the mixture to cook until it is slightly thickened and syrupy. Remove from the heat and allow it to cool completely.

TO ASSEMBLE Slice braised bacon lengthwise into ½-inch slices, and cut each slice into 3 pieces. In a pan on medium heat, cook the bacon until golden brown and crispy.

Remove bacon from the pan, retaining bacon fat. Toast baguette slices in the bacon fat. Flip and cook until they are golden on both sides.

Spread 1 tsp of mayo on each toasted baguette and top with one piece of bacon. Finish with a drizzle of gastrique, a dollop of compote, and a bit more gastrique. Repeat for as many crostini as you want to serve.

Ingredients continued overleaf

PIRI PIRI SAUCE
5 medium jalapeño peppers
3 cloves garlic
1 Tbsp smoked paprika
½ cup fresh lime juice
1 Tbsp red wine vinegar
¾ cup extra-virgin olive oil
Kosher salt

PIPERADE
⅓ cup olive oil
½ white onion, thinly sliced lengthwise
½ red onion, thinly sliced lengthwise
1 red pepper, cut lengthwise into
¼-inch strips
1 yellow pepper, cut lengthwise into
¼-inch strips

5 cloves garlic, roughly chopped
4 tomatoes, cored and diced
(¼-inch cubes)
Kosher salt
Piment d'esplette (or cayenne),
to taste

SERVES 4

Chorizo and Piri Piri Shrimp Paella

*Paella, as Cosmo Kramer colourfully put it in a **Seinfeld** episode, is a Spanish "orgiastic feast for the senses, a wanton festival of sights, sounds, and colours." Of course, Corey's version has added some chefy touches: a **piperade**, which is a Basque Country sauté of tomatoes and peppers, and a **gremolata**, an Italian herby, lemony condiment. These components are easier to make than they sound and add layers of flavour to this mélange of fish, meat, and rice. Very tasty.*

PIRI PIRI SAUCE Preheat the oven to 500°F. Roast jalapeños on a baking sheet until blackened all over and soft, 10 to 15 minutes.

Allow jalapeños to cool, then trim stems, cut in half, and remove seeds and white ribs. (Leave the blackened skin on.)

To a blender, add jalapeños, garlic, paprika, lime juice, and vinegar. Blend until smooth. Add olive oil and a bit of salt and blend again for about 1 minute.

PIPERADE Heat a large saucepan on medium. Add olive oil and allow it to get hot enough that you see ripples in it. Add onions, peppers, garlic, and tomatoes. Cook, stirring occasionally, for about 10 minutes, or until vegetables are softened and begin to brown. Remove from the heat and allow to cool. Season to taste with salt and piment d'esplette (or whatever hot pepper you have around).

Recipe continued overleaf

GREMOLATA AIOLI

2 lemons
2 egg yolks
4 cloves garlic, passed through
a fine grater or zester
1 tsp salt
1 tsp honey
1 ½ cups canola oil
½ cup chopped parsley
Freshly ground black pepper

PAELLA

1 lb large shrimp, peeled and deveined
¼ cup piri piri sauce
1 Tbsp extra-virgin olive oil
1 white onion, finely diced
1 cup chopped mushrooms
of your choice
2 cups carnaroli rice

Pinch of saffron threads
Salt and freshly ground black pepper
1 cup white wine
8 cups vegetable or chicken stock
2 Tbsp butter
9 oz dry chorizo (or Andouille)
sausage, cut into ⅛-inch slices

GREMOLATA AIOLI Peel only the yellow part of each lemon's zest and then juice them. Blanch lemon zest in boiling water for 5 seconds, then strain and allow to cool.

In a food processor, combine egg yolks, half of the lemon juice, garlic, salt, and honey. Blend until thickened and frothy. Add lemon zest and pulse a few times. With the food processor running, slowly pour in oil to form an emulsion. If it's too thick, add more lemon juice to thin mixture or to your taste.

Scrape aioli into a bowl and fold in parsley. Adjust seasoning with salt and pepper to taste.

PAELLA Butterfly shrimp by piercing through the middle of the shrimp (where the vein used to be) about three-quarters of the way through, and then slicing all the way down to the tail. Marinate in piri piri sauce for 2 hours.

Preheat the oven to 400°F.

In a large saucepan, heat olive oil on medium. Add onions and mushrooms. Cook until soft, about 3 minutes.

Add rice and stir until all of the grains are coated with oil and begin to brown slightly. Add saffron threads and a large pinch of salt and pepper. Stir to combine. Add white wine and stir until it comes to a simmer. Then slowly add stock, 1 cup at a time, stirring continuously to incorporate before adding the next cup, similar to making risotto.

Keep adding stock until rice is soft and fully cooked, with just a little bite to it. Remove from the heat and stir in butter.

Spoon rice into a 16-inch round paella dish (or any ovenproof casserole pan) and spread evenly. Place piperade onto the centre of the dish in a pile and arrange shrimp in a circle around the piperade. Then arrange chorizo slices around the outside edge of the shrimp. Season with a pinch of salt and pepper.

Bake until shrimp are cooked and sausage and piperade are heated through, 10 to 15 minutes.

Garnish with a zigzag of gremolata aioli all over the dish and serve hot.

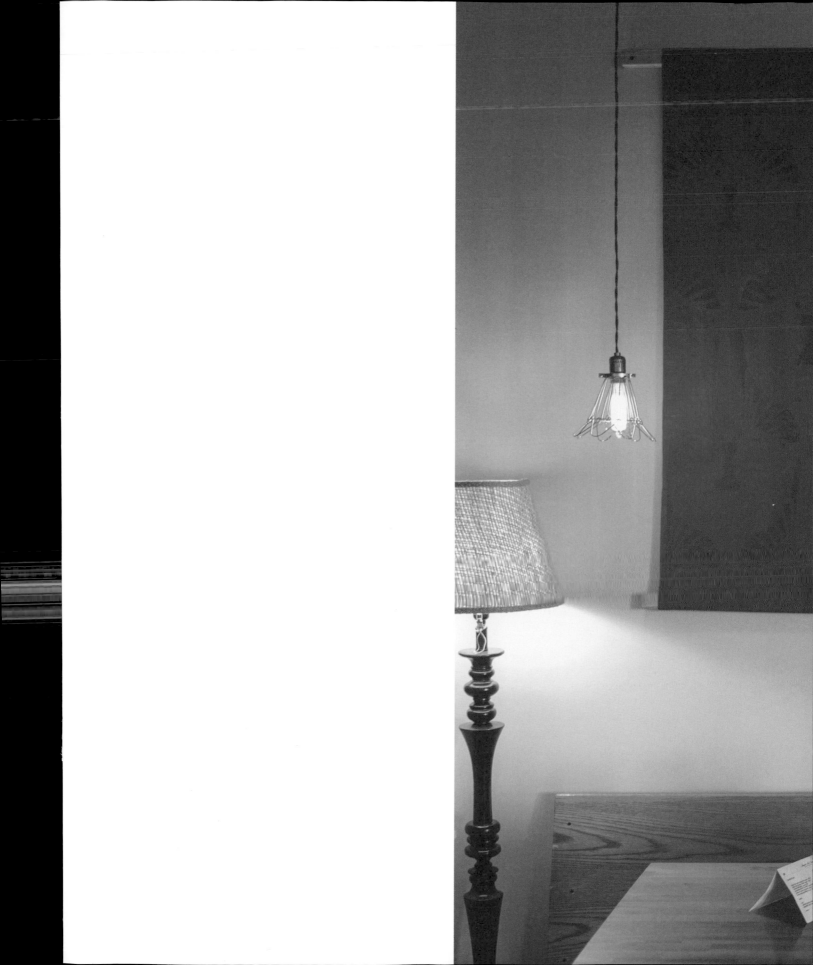

Under the High Wheel

JENNIFER OGLE
▪ *owner & chef* ▪

ADA KALINOWSKI
▪ *owner* ▪

In the new-but-made-to-look-old Roots on Whyte building is a whole community of people who walk the walk when it comes to the support-local, organic ethos. And on its main floor, Under the High Wheel — owned and operated by close friends Jennifer Ogle and Ada Kalinowski (left and right, respectively) — serves the kind of food I love to eat: flavourful and honest, made with our local harvest.

The space is airy and the ceilings high. Brick walls and industrial lighting give it edge, while upcycled church pews and antique tapestries give it warmth. Brunch is served all day, every day, a welcome liberation from the shackles of

the weekend. A standout offering? Organic sweet and savoury crepes and fluffy Belgian waffles, crowned with Chantilly cream and berries or as the base of smoked salmon eggs benny.

I suppress a child-like tantrum when the Roasted Beet and Orange Salad is not in the deli case of rotating salads. And I almost always order the Croque Monsieur — a meal more than a sandwich, made with slices of roasted Four Whistle Farms pork, caramelized apples, and velvety béchamel oozing all over organic Boulangerie Bonjour Bakery bread — and am almost always surprised by how I've not tired of it yet.

But when I want a meal that feels like a hug from the inside, one that soothes aching bones and lifts heavy hearts, I devour Jennifer's Bangers and Mash — sweet caramelized onions, local cranberry maple sausage, and a deeply savoury veal demi — it's English pub fare elevated to refined comfort food befitting her French culinary training.

Vegan, vegetarian, and gluten-free meals are just as delicious here, an egalitarian quest for taste, made with local, seasonal food that nourishes the body and supports the community. A winning combination indeed. — **TF**

6 medium beets
2 Tbsp sunflower oil
1 tsp salt
1 tsp freshly ground black pepper
2 oranges, preferably Valencia

ORANGE AND HONEY DRESSING

1 cup orange juice (use juice saved from segmenting oranges)
1 Tbsp honey
⅓ cup white balsamic vinegar
½ cup sunflower oil
Salt and freshly ground black pepper

ASSEMBLY

4 oz goat cheese (optional)
Pecans, hazelnuts, or walnuts, toasted and chopped (optional)

SERVES 4-6

Roasted Beet and Orange Salad

SALAD Preheat the oven to 400°F.

Arrange beets on a large baking sheet. Drizzle with oil, salt, and pepper and toss to coat. Cover the sheet with aluminum foil and bake for 45 to 60 minutes or until the beets can be easily stuck with a fork. Remove foil and allow beets to cool for 15 minutes. When beets are cool, peel them and cut them into wedges.

Cut the top and bottom off of the oranges. Place the cut side down on a cutting board and, using a sharp paring knife, remove the peel in vertical sections. Working over a bowl (to catch juice for the dressing), cut each segment away from the membranes around it. Squeeze as much juice as you can from the membranes into the bowl before discarding.

ORANGE AND HONEY DRESSING In a bowl, whisk together orange juice, honey, vinegar, and sunflower oil. Season with salt and pepper to taste. This will make more dressing than you'll need. Store it in a sealed Mason jar in the fridge for future salads.

TO ASSEMBLE In a large salad bowl, toss beets and oranges together with dressing to taste. Crumble goat cheese and nuts (if using) overtop.

3 large Yukon gold potatoes

2 Tbsp butter
2 large yellow onions, julienned
1 Tbsp balsamic vinegar
Leaves of 1 sprig fresh thyme
Salt and freshly ground pepper

SERVES **2**

Bangers and Mash

The beef bone **jus,** *which has the consistency of luscious gravy and flavour of a real demi-glace, truly makes this dish. Its deep savouriness comes from two days of patiently concentrating flavours of roasted bones, vegetables, herbs, and wine. (Those seeking immediate satisfaction can buy the jus from Under the High Wheel.) Bangers and Mash are comforting on a blizzardy Sunday morning, after a night of heavy imbibing — and, of course, anytime you have leftover mashed potatoes.*

MASHED POTATOES Peel and cut potatoes into large chunks. Place potatoes in pot and cover with salted water. Bring to a boil and simmer until tender, 15 to 20 minutes. Drain. Mash potatoes using a food mill or a potato ricer. Potatoes can be refrigerated for a day or two at this stage and reheated when you're ready to serve.

CARAMELIZED ONIONS In a frying pan on medium-high heat, melt butter. Add onions, stirring often until they start to brown and caramelize. Lower heat to medium-low, add vinegar and thyme, and cook, stirring often, for 20 to 30 minutes, until onions are a rich caramel colour and silky and tender. If onions stick to the pan during cooking, add a bit of water or stock to deglaze. Season to taste with salt and pepper. Set aside.

ROASTED BONE JUS

8 ½–9 lbs veal or beef bones
⅓ cup honey
2 carrots, roughly chopped
2 onions, roughly chopped
2 ribs celery, roughly chopped
1 can (12 oz) tomato paste
2 cups water
6 sprigs parsley
3 bay leaves
1 tsp whole black peppercorns
1 cup red wine

ASSEMBLY

6 farmers' market sausages
(Under the High Wheel uses
Pembina cranberry maple sausages)
4 eggs
3 Tbsp unsalted butter
3 Tbsp whipping (35%) cream
Salt and freshly ground black pepper
Pea shoots, microgreens, or finely
chopped parsley, for garnish

ROASTED BONE JUS Preheat the oven to 400°F. Place bones in a roasting pan and roast in the oven until lightly browned, about 30 minutes. Add honey, carrots, onions, celery, and tomato paste to the pan. Roast bones and vegetables until they are a rich brown colour and caramelized, about 25 minutes.

Transfer bones and vegetables to a large stockpot. Deglaze the roasting pan with water (you can use wine if you have extra lying around) and add juices to the stockpot.

Add parsley, bay leaves, peppercorns, and enough cold water to cover the bones and vegetables.

Cook stock on medium heat until it starts to bubble, then reduce heat to a simmer for 12 to 16 hours. Be sure to skim the fat and impurities that come to the surface frequently and continue to add more cold water as needed to keep the bones covered.

When ready, strain the stock through a colander, then strain again with a colander lined with cheesecloth. Refrigerate overnight. Skim the fat layer off the stock and pour stock in a pot along with red wine. Heat stock on medium until reduced by half, anywhere from 1 to 3 hours. This jus freezes well.

TO ASSEMBLE Cook sausages and eggs to your favourite style.

Heat 2 cups of roasted bone jus.

When ready to eat, heat mashed potatoes in a pot with butter and cream. When piping hot, season to taste with salt and pepper.

Warm 2 plates in the oven. When all of your elements are hot, place one large scoop of mash and 2 Tbsp caramelized onions side by side on one-third of the plate. Place eggs in the middle and nestle bangers on the mashed potatoes. Spoon a generous amount of roasted bone jus over the potatoes and bangers, being careful not to get any on the eggs. Garnish with pea shoots, microgreens, or finely chopped parsley. Serve hot.

Uccellino

DANIEL COSTA
▪ *owner* ▪

ALLEN ANDERL
▪ *front-of-house manager* ▪

CHRISTOPHER HYDE
▪ *chef* ▪

With the opening of Uccellino in 2016, Daniel Costa (right) completed his trilogy of Italian restaurants, built literally next door to one another on a colourful stretch of Jasper Avenue. This, his largest yet, is a light-filled, 80-seat modern rendition of a *trattoria:* a neighbourhood haunt where you sink into a comforting bowl of pasta and a juicy red— and don't pay a fortune for it.

"It's the kind of food I love to eat, the kind of food I make at home," Daniel says, almost unable to contain his fervour. "It's why I go to Italy, to eat this food. I'm obsessed with making the perfect Amatriciana."

That spicy tomatoey mess of pasta is the core of Uccellino's unchefy menu of unadulterated classics like pasta carbonara and *cacio e pepe* (literally, cheese and pepper emulsified into a luscious creamy sauce) — minimalist dishes that, seemingly for hundreds of years, have remained doggedly immune to the culinary trends that have influenced the rest of the world.

A month before opening, Daniel, front-of-house manager Allen Anderl (left) and chef Christopher Hyde (centre) went to Italy for a research binge, eating six kinds of Amatriciana to learn how it's done, to get inspired, and to solidify the concept: it's fresh, seasonal ingredients cooked simply to make the most of the quality and flavours.

Take a T-bone steak. They'll char it and serve it with a bottle of olive oil and lemon. That's it. Pair it with a big, leathery Brunello, and it's that purity of flavours that beats fussy, complicated cooking any day.

The place is open all day for lunch, dinner, or a late dinner. Go on, eat something great.

3 Tbsp extra-virgin olive oil, plus more for finishing
½ lb pancetta, finely diced
2 carrots, finely diced
4 ribs celery, finely diced
½ onion, finely diced
6 fresh sage leaves
Salt and freshly ground black pepper

2 cloves garlic, minced
3 Tbsp double-concentrated tomato paste
1 cup dry white wine
2 cups semi-pearled farro
6 cups chicken stock
2 large handfuls fresh spinach
1 tsp red wine vinegar

SERVES **4**

Farro Soup

Farro is an ancient grain, an heirloom variety of wheat often mistaken for spelt. It's nutty and slightly sweet, with a satisfying chew. Said to have been found in tombs of Egyptian kings, farro was later brought to Italy (where it was called "pharaoh's wheat") and used to feed Roman legions. And it can be on your table in about 45 minutes with Daniel's hearty soup, where it adds a pleasing al dente bite to the softened vegetables.

Tip: Farro comes in two versions: whole grain, which requires an overnight soak, or semi-pearled (semiperlato in Italian), where some of its bran has been removed, making it easy to cook in a half-hour.

HEAT OLIVE OIL in a medium, heavy-bottomed pot on medium-high. Once oil is shimmering, add pancetta and cook until golden brown, 3 to 5 minutes. Add carrots, celery, onions, and sage, and season with pinch of salt and pepper. Cook until vegetables begin to colour, about 5 minutes. Add garlic and cook for another 4 minutes. Add tomato paste, stir to combine, and cook for 1 minute. Add white wine and cook for 2 minutes. Add farro and chicken stock.

Turn heat down to a simmer. Cook until farro is tender, about 25 minutes. Stir occasionally and add more broth if you prefer your soup a little thinner.

Once farro is tender, stir in spinach and cook for 1 minute. Remove from the heat, add vinegar, and season to taste with salt and pepper. Serve in bowls with a drizzle of olive oil.

1 **Tbsp** extra-virgin olive oil

8 **oz** guanciale (or pancetta), cut into thick matchsticks

1 **can** (28 oz) San Marzano tomatoes, crushed by hand

1 **Tbsp** chili flakes

1 **tsp** kosher salt

1 **lb** dry bucatini

¾ **cup** Pecorino Romano, finely grated, plus more for garnish

SERVES **4**

Bucatini all'Amatriciana

This seven-ingredient wonder is Daniel's brilliant take on a classic spicy tomato pasta named after the town of Amatrice, about an hour east of Rome. He tosses the long, hollow pasta strands (bucatini) with smoky guanciale (Italian salt-cured pork jowl) and doesn't hold back on the chili flakes. The guanciale makes all the difference, but if you can't find it, use pancetta instead. Pair this with good red wine—Italian, of course. Daniel suggests Chianti, Rosso Piceno, or Aglianico.

HEAT OLIVE OIL in a large frying pan on medium-high heat. Add guanciale and cook until the fat has rendered out and the meat is golden, about 5 minutes. Remove guanciale from the pan and set aside on a plate. To the same pan, add crushed tomatoes, chili flakes, and salt. Cook for 10 minutes, stirring frequently.

While tomatoes are cooking, bring a large pot of salted water to a boil. Cook bucatini until al dente (about 1 minute less than package instructions). Once pasta is cooked, reserve 1 cup of pasta cooking water. Drain pasta, or, using tongs, simply drag pasta into the frying pan with the tomato sauce. Return tomato sauce to high heat and add half of the reserved pasta cooking water. The residual starch in that water will thicken the sauce. Cook for about 1 minute or until the liquid is thick and coating the pasta. Remove pan from the heat. Stir in guanciale and Pecorino Romano. Add a little more pasta water if the sauce is too stiff. You want a fluid, creamy texture.

Serve immediately with a fresh snowing of Pecorino Romano.

vivo
ristorante

MICHAEL HASSALL
▪ chef ▪

Far from the trendy foodie tracts of 104 and 124 Streets, in a non-descript west-end strip-mall, lives vivo ristorante—a refuge of locally sourced, lovingly made rustic Italian food amid the vapid restaurant chains and fast-food outlets that surround it.

Head chef Michael Hassall's food is all served family style, meaning your party will have to agree on what to order, and is made to be enjoyed in the classic Italian way—over several courses and, naturally, several glasses of wine.

You begin with *antipasti* (appetizers), and you'd be a fool not to try Hassall's Caprese salad, upped a notch with house-made pesto,

candy-like semi sun-dried tomatoes, balsamic glaze, and crunchy bursts of coarse grey sea salt. Next is *primi* (the pasta course), all of which is made fresh in-house, but the pan-fried, crispy, light-as-clouds gnocchi are particularly delicious. Leave room for *secondi* (the main course), such as juicy rib steak with pear and arugula, or half a roasted duck with fig balsamic vinegar, grilled lime, and radicchio—equal parts sweet, savoury, tart, and bitter.

The meats are heaped on showy wood cutting boards, with rolling foothills of *contorni* (vegetable sides), where humble Brussels sprouts—with a hit of spicy honey, pancetta,

and a few minutes in a blazing clay oven— become charred morsels of sweet-savoury bliss.

Everyone digs in, and you quickly feel as though you're sitting at your own kitchen table, with the added joy of stumbling home without washing a single dish. *Buonanotte!*

GNOCCHI
2 cups ricotta, as dry as possible
½ cup all-purpose flour
2 medium egg yolks
1 tsp sea salt

WALNUT BUTTER
1 cup walnuts
2 Tbsp honey
1 Tbsp extra-virgin olive oil

ASSEMBLY
2 Tbsp butter
5–7 large sage leaves
2 Tbsp walnut butter
1 Tbsp extra-virgin olive oil, plus more for finishing

Pecorino Romano, to taste, for finishing
Salt and freshly ground black pepper

SERVES **2-4**

Ricotta Gnocchi
with Walnut Brown Butter and Crispy Sage

GNOCCHI Wrap ricotta in a cheesecloth and hang overnight in fridge, with a bowl underneath to catch any drippings. Discard drippings.

Bring a small pot with 4 cups salted water to a boil. Meanwhile, using a stand mixer fitted with a dough hook, mix ricotta, flour, egg yolks, and salt on medium speed for 5 minutes.

Take a tablespoon-sized piece of dough and roll into a cylinder, about half the size of a cork. Add to the boiling water and cook until the gnoccho has been floating for 30 seconds — this is to test the dough to make sure it has enough flour.

Taste the gnoccho. Add ¼ cup more flour and mix for 1 minute if the gnoccho does not hold its shape. Roll dough into snake-like lengths — about as long as your cutting board and the thickness of a cork — and cut into ½-inch segments, lightly dusting with flour as you go.

Place a single layer of gnocchi on a baking sheet lined with parchment paper and freeze. Once frozen, store in a sealed zipper bag. These will keep for up to 2 months in the freezer.

WALNUT BUTTER Soak walnuts overnight in cold water to help remove tannins.

Preheat the oven to 350°F. Drain and dry walnuts, then toast on a baking sheet in the oven for 8 minutes, until golden brown. Remove walnuts from the oven and allow them to cool until you can touch them with your hands. Using a mortar and pestle, crush and blend walnuts, honey, and oil until they form a paste.

TO ASSEMBLE Bring a large pot of salted water to a boil. Add frozen gnocchi and give a quick stir. The gnocchi are done when they have been floating for about 30 seconds. Drain gnocchi and set aside.

Add butter to a frying pan on medium heat. When it has been cooking for about 1 minute, add sage. Fry until butter has turned brown — you now have crispy sage and brown butter. Add 2 Tbsp walnut butter and set the pan aside. Taste and add salt as needed.

In a separate non-stick frying pan, bring olive oil up to medium heat, then turn the heat up to medium-high and fry the cooked gnocchi, turning and tossing until a golden-brown crust forms on the outside. Taste and add salt as needed.

To plate the dish, use a deep bowl and place the fried gnocchi in the bottom. Over it, pour the walnut, brown butter, and sage mixture. Garnish with freshly shaved Pecorino Romano (the more aged, the better). Garnish with a drizzle of olive oil and serve.

Just a few ingredients and some patience are all you need to make Michael's airy, delightfully creamy gnocchi. And the better-quality those ingredients, the better your final product. At vivo, they use top-notch local provisions, including Four Whistle Farm eggs, Beanstalk Honey, Steve and Dan's Fresh BC walnuts, Vancouver Island sea salt, and Nefiss Lezizz olive oil.

MANGALITSA PANCETTA TESA

¼ **cup** fine sea salt

3 **Tbsp** roughly cracked black peppercorns

¼ **cup** dried juniper berries

8 **cloves** garlic, minced

8 bay leaves, crumbled

8 **sprigs** fresh rosemary

1 Mangalitsa pork belly (10 lbs), skin on

2 **cups** white wine

ANATRA

1 duck, 5–6 lbs

2 **Tbsp** olive oil

1 cinnamon stick

1 **Tbsp** dried juniper berries

1 **Tbsp** whole black peppercorns

2 **sprigs** fresh rosemary

2 **sprigs** fresh thyme

3 bay leaves

1 white onion, diced

2 medium carrots, diced

2 **ribs** celery, diced

1 orange, cut into quarters

1 **bulb** garlic, cloves split apart and peeled

1 **cup** white wine

8 ¼ **cups** chicken stock

SERVES **1-2**

Anatra *(Duck)* with *Sorrel Pesto*
and *Cavoletti di Bruxelles (Brussels Sprouts)*

Michael cures his own pancetta. It takes four weeks for the entire process. He also makes his own spiced honey. That takes two days for the flavours to infuse. Both recipes are included here, but if you'd like to eat this for dinner tonight — and we don't blame you — use regular honey and pick up pancetta from your neighbourhood deli or butcher. If you have the time and inclination to shop locally, these are Michael's sources for this recipe: Country Accent for Mangalitsa pork, Four Whistle Farm for duck, and Riverbend Gardens and Sundog Organic Farm for herbs and veggies.

MANGALITSA PANCETTA TESA Combine salt, peppercorns, juniper berries, garlic, bay leaves, and rosemary in a non-reactive container large enough to hold all ingredients. Add pork belly and rub ingredients all over. Refrigerate for 5 days, flipping and redistributing the ingredients each day. After 5 days, remove belly and rinse off salt and herbs under white wine.

(You may not need both cups.) Hang belly with butcher's twine in cool, dark place for 3 to 4 weeks.

ANATRA Using a sharp knife, separate the two duck breasts, wings, and legs. Score the fat on the skin side of the breast, being careful not to cut into the flesh of the duck. Set breasts aside in the fridge until assembly.

Meanwhile, add olive oil to a heavy-bottomed stainless steel pot that can hold 1 gallon of liquid and set on high heat. Sear duck wings and legs until skin is golden brown; remove and set aside.

To the same pot, add cinnamon stick, juniper berries, peppercorns, rosemary, thyme, bay leaves, onions, carrots, celery, orange, and garlic and cook for 2 minutes. Add white wine and reduce by half, then add chicken stock. Add legs and wings back into the pot, and, if there is room, add any leftover parts from the duck, such as the carcass or neck, to make the stock even richer.

SORREL PESTO

2 cloves black garlic, minced
1 Tbsp grainy mustard
4 Tbsp extra-virgin olive oil, divided
2 Tbsp sunflower seeds, toasted
1 Tbsp grated Parmigiano Reggiano
¼ cup packed sorrel
1 tsp coarse grey sea salt

SPICY DANDELION HONEY

4 cups dandelion honey
4 Tbsp Marash pepper
(from a medium-heat Turkish
chili pepper — or use harissa)

CAVOLETTI DI BRUXELLES

2 cups Brussels sprouts, halved
2–3 Tbsp olive oil
5–6 thin slices pancetta
Spicy dandelion honey, to taste

Bring to a simmer and cook on low heat for about 2 hours. To check if the duck is ready, test a wing; it ought to be "falling apart" tender. Carefully pull the other wing and legs out and reserve. Strain stock and keep for another use.

SORREL PESTO Using a mortar and pestle, crush the black garlic, mustard, 2 Tbsp of the olive oil, sunflower seeds, and Parmigiano Reggiano until finely ground. Add sorrel and salt. Mix until a paste has formed, and add remaining 2 Tbsp olive oil. Keeps for 1 to 2 days in the fridge.

SPICY DANDELION HONEY In a heatproof bowl over a pot of gently simmering water (or in the top of a double boiler), heat the honey until it is just runny. Take it off the heat, add Marash pepper, and allow to sit for 48 hours.

CAVOLETTI DI BRUXELLES Preheat the oven to 400°F.

Toss Brussels sprouts in olive oil and place on a baking sheet. Top with pancetta slices. The fat that melts from the pancetta will help to cook the sprouts in a sort of confit style.

Roast in oven for about 15 minutes, or until golden and soft through the core. Place on a serving platter and drizzle with spicy honey, to taste.

TO ASSEMBLE To a non-stick pan on medium heat, add duck breasts, skin-side down. Reduce heat to low and cook until 70 percent of the fat has rendered out, 10 to 14 minutes. Flip duck and continue to cook until internal temperature reads 110°F on a meat thermometer.

Meanwhile (about halfway through cooking the duck breasts, and while the Brussels sprouts are roasting), reheat the wings and leg in the oven with a little of the braising stock — this will help keep them moist.

When breasts are cooked, remove from the heat and place on a cutting board. Allow them to rest for 5 minutes. Slice breasts on an angle and place neatly with legs, wings, and Brussels sprouts on a serving platter. Finish with sorrel pesto, coarse grey sea salt, and a drizzle of olive oil.

Zaika Indian Bistro

JOTI DHANJU
▪ *owner* ▪

Inside Zaika, the room is dark and sultry, with hits of sparkle and modern lights befitting a sleek Vegas bar. Despite its contemporary interior, there's no mistaking that you've walked into an Indian restaurant: the warm aroma of spices instantly surrounds you, and the slapping sounds of naan dough being stretched before it enters the hot clay tandoor is enough to set your mouth watering.

The star of Zaika's predominantly northern Indian menu is the beloved Mango Chicken, on the menu since day one. You can get lost in its wonderfully luxurious sweet-savoury cream sauce, perfect for sopping up with pieces of

hot, buttery naan. It also happens to be one of the milder dishes on the menu. Prepare to have your senses jolted by chef Ansuya Prasad's incendiary vindaloos and sinus-clearing masalas. It takes a few bites before the chilies kick in. Then, watch out: your eyes widen, your lips tingle, and your cheeks flush as your temperature rises. For relief, order a refreshing mango lassi (a cooling yogurt-based smoothie), or tame the heat with one of three Indian beers on offer.

Cap off your meal with a sweet dessert to diffuse the heat and balance the senses. Gulab jamun (sweet milk dumplings in rosewater-spiked syrup) are delectable and addictive, as is the cardamom rice pudding. Neither is complete without a pot of aromatic masala chai, strongly brewed black tea simmered with milk, cardamom, and cinnamon, poured from high up to create froth and release its flavours. It's enjoyed all across the country, from the deserts of Rajasthan to the seaside megacity of Mumbai—and, of course, right here in Edmonton.

4 chicken breasts, skinless

Salt and freshly ground black pepper

2 Tbsp + **1 tsp** canola or vegetable oil, divided

4 white onions, very finely diced

1 cup tomato paste

4 mangoes, roughly chopped

4 Tbsp ground coriander seeds

1 tsp ground cumin

1 tsp ground turmeric

2 tsp salt

3 Tbsp minced fresh ginger

2 cups whipping (35%) cream

Julienned fresh ginger, for garnish

Chopped green onions, for garnish

SERVES **4**

Mango Chicken

PREHEAT the oven to 350°F. Season chicken breasts with a pinch of salt and pepper and bake in an ovenproof dish for 15 to 20 minutes, until they reach an internal temperature of 165°F. Allow to cool, then dice the breasts into 1- to 2-inch pieces for later use. Set aside.

Heat 2 Tbsp of the oil in a large sauté pan on medium. Add onions and gently sweat for about 10 minutes or until they become translucent and soft. Allow onions to cool slightly, then purée in a food processor.

Add tomato paste, mangoes, coriander, cumin, turmeric, and salt. Blend until the sauce is creamy and thick.

In a medium saucepan on medium, sweat the ginger with the remaining 1 tsp oil until it becomes translucent. Add chicken and mango purée and heat, stirring gently. Add cream and simmer for at least 15 minutes. Garnish with julienned ginger and green onions. Adjust seasoning with salt and pepper to taste and serve with basmati rice and naan.

4 Tbsp canola oil
2 tsp ginger paste or minced fresh ginger
2 tsp garlic paste or minced fresh garlic
1 lb boneless lamb, cut into 2-inch cubes
4 tomatoes, puréed
3 onions, boiled and puréed
1 tsp ground turmeric

1 tsp ground coriander seeds
½ tsp ground cumin
1 tsp paprika
1 tsp salt
¼ tsp freshly ground black pepper
½ cup + **2 Tbsp** whipping (35%) cream
2 ¾ cups water

1 ½ cups basmati rice
5 cloves, whole
1 cinnamon stick, broken in half
⅓ cup cashews, chopped
⅓ cup raisins
Chopped cilantro, for garnish

SERVES **4**

Lamb Biryani

HEAT OIL in a medium saucepan on medium. Add ginger and garlic, and sweat for several minutes, being careful not to burn the garlic. Add lamb and cook until it's browned and slightly caramelized on all sides, 5 to 8 minutes. Add tomatoes, onions, turmeric, coriander, cumin, paprika, salt, and pepper. Allow to simmer, uncovered, until the lamb is fully cooked, about 20 minutes. Add cream and simmer for another 3 to 4 minutes on medium heat.

While the lamb is cooking, cook the rice. In a large pot, combine water, rice, and a pinch of salt. Bring to a boil on high heat; then reduce heat, cover, and cook for 15 minutes.

Once the rice is cooked, add cloves and cinnamon stick, and fluff rice slightly with a fork. Adjust seasoning to taste with salt and pepper.

On medium heat, add lamb to the rice, mixing thoroughly with a wooden spoon. Taste and adjust seasoning again. Top with chopped cashews and raisins. Add chopped cilantro for extra colour and flavour.

Conversion Charts

VOLUME

IMPERIAL	METRIC
⅛ tsp	0.5 mL
¼ tsp	1 mL
½ tsp	2.5 mL
¾ tsp	4 mL
1 tsp	5 mL
½ Tbsp	8 mL
1 Tbsp	15 mL
1 ½ Tbsp	23 mL
2 Tbsp	30 mL
¼ cup	60 mL
⅓ cup	80 mL
½ cup	125 mL
⅔ cup	165 mL
¾ cup	185 mL
1 cup	250 mL
1 ¼ cups	310 mL
1 ⅓ cups	330 mL
1 ½ cups	375 mL
1 ⅔ cups	415 mL
1 ¾ cups	435 mL
2 cups	500 mL
2 ¼ cups	560 mL
2 ⅓ cups	580 mL
2 ½ cups	625 mL
2 ¾ cups	690 mL
3 cups	750 mL
4 cups/1 qt	1 L
5 cups	1.25 L
6 cups	1.5 L
7 cups	1.75 L
8 cups	2 L

CANS & JARS

IMPERIAL	METRIC
6 oz	170 g
28 oz	796 mL

WEIGHT

IMPERIAL	METRIC
½ oz	15 g
1 oz	30 g
2 oz	60 g
3 oz	85 g
4 oz (¼ lb)	115 g
5 oz	140 g
6 oz	170 g
7 oz	200 g
8 oz (½ lb)	225 g
9 oz	255 g
10 oz	285 g
11 oz	310 g
12 oz (¾ lb)	340 g
13 oz	370 g
14 oz	400 g
15 oz	425 g
16 oz (1 lb)	450 g
1 ¼ lbs	570 g
1 ½ lbs	670 g
2 lbs	900 g
3 lbs	1.4 kg
4 lbs	1.8 kg
5 lbs	2.3 kg
6 lbs	2.7 kg

LIQUID MEASURES

IMPERIAL	METRIC
1 fl oz	30 mL
2 fl oz	60 mL
3 fl oz	90 mL
4 fl oz	120 mL

LINEAR

IMPERIAL	METRIC
⅛ inch	3 mm
¼ inch	6 mm
½ inch	12 mm
¾ inch	2 cm
1 inch	2.5 cm
1 ¼ inches	3 cm
1 ½ inches	3.5 cm
1 ¾ inches	4.5 cm
2 inches	5 cm
2 ½ inches	6.5 cm
3 inches	7.5 cm
4 inches	10 cm
5 inches	12.5 cm
6 inches	15 cm
7 inches	18 cm
10 inches	25 cm
12 inches/1 foot	30 cm
13 inches	33 cm
16 inches	41 cm
18 inches	46 cm
24 inches/2 feet	60 cm
28 inches	70 cm
30 inches	75 cm
6 feet	1.8 m

BAKING PANS

IMPERIAL	METRIC
5 × 9-inch loaf pan	2 L loaf pan
9 × 13-inch cake pan	4 L cake pan
11 × 17-inch baking sheet	30 × 45-cm baking sheet

TEMPERATURE

IMPERIAL	METRIC
90°F	32°C
120°F	49°C
125°F	52°C
130°F	54°C
140°F	60°C
150°F	66°C
155°F	68°C
160°F	71°C
165°F	74°C
170°F	77°C
175°F	80°C
180°F	82°C
190°F	88°C
200°F	93°C
240°F	116°C
250°F	121°C
300°F	149°C
325°F	163°C
350°F	177°C
360°F	182°C
375°F	191°C

OVEN TEMPERATURE

IMPERIAL	METRIC
200°F	95°C
250°F	120°C
275°F	135°C
300°F	150°C
325°F	160°C
350°F	180°C
375°F	190°C
400°F	200°C
425°F	220°C
450°F	230°C

Acknowledgements

Though our names appear on the cover, there is a small army of wildly talented creatives we've been truly lucky to work with over the 18 months it took to create the cookbook you're holding in your hands.

First, this book would not be possible without our visionary publisher, Chris Labonté of Figure 1. Thank you, Chris, for approaching us about this project and for your deep belief that Edmonton's culinary landscape is worth celebrating. You let us choose the restaurants and highlight Edmonton's culinary diversity. We bonded over this belief and are thrilled with the final product.

The daily realities of writing, editing (six rounds), photographing (over 1,000 photos), and designing (over 200 pages) this book (and, okay, a bit of eating, too) were expertly managed by the intrepid Lara Smith. She kept us all on schedule, focused, and delivering our best in true superhero fashion. Thank you Chris, Lara, and the entire Figure 1 family for taking us on this wonderful journey (and keeping us on deadline)!

Our heartfelt appreciation goes to our brilliant editor, Linda Pruessen, for her thoughtful and thorough observations, her warmth and kindness as she made sense of a sea of notes, and her incredible talent at shaping unwieldy text into clear prose, like a masterful bread baker forming her dough. It's been a true pleasure working with her.

We eat with our eyes first, and Dong Kim's dazzling, mouth-watering photography made us all hungry. We won't be surprised if it makes you drool a little, too. Under the gifted art direction of Jess Sullivan, this book is a true feast for the eyes. Thank you to the talented Natalie Olsen, whose love of typography and the printed page is infectious and evident in every perfectly laid-out page before you.

Thanks, too, to Iva Cheung for her meticulous copy editing and great wit.

And to Mark Redmayne and his team for working to spread the word and get *Edmonton Cooks* out there.

We will be forever in debt to the great connector, Marilyn Hooper, for introducing us. Two like minds can make something much greater together. Thank you!

And finally, a heartfelt thanks to the army of chefs and restaurateurs in this book for generously sharing their craft and secret recipes from their coveted kitchens. The publishing process is demanding, but you managed it with grace while running a busy restaurant. Thank you for helping us celebrate you!

And above all else, we want to thank you, dear reader, for buying this book and supporting Edmonton's exciting independent restaurants. With this we celebrate our city's food culture, its diversity, and the farmers, artisans, and chefs who make our home — our beautiful Edmonton — a wonderful city to live in. Time to eat!

Like most people, my love of food comes from my family. My earliest memories of cooking are beside my grandmother's apron strings, whisking eggs for an omelette, or whipping honey butter with my grandfather and slathering it on fresh, hot Iranian flatbread from the bakery down the street.

I grew up in an epicurean family, amid fruit trees and laying hens. My brothers and I would shake the apricot tree loose of its green, unripe fruit, and eat it with a snowy sprinkle of salt—the ultimate Persian after-school snack. My mom regularly prepared tongue and brain long before offal was trendy, and I still cannot get enough of my dad's fesenjoon and fried-egg sandwiches. Alluring flavours of rosewater, persimmons, pomegranates, saffron, and barberries are the alphabet of my childhood culinary education. I wholly owe my love of and curiosity about food, what it means, and how to generously share it, to this upbringing, my dear parents, and elder brothers. It's a lifelong pursuit, and I'm grateful for their profound influence.

My dear husband, Robert Andruchow, encourages me daily to be my best self, in writing and in life, and I am eternally thankful for his unending love and support.

I'd also like to thank all the editors and producers (too many to name here) who, over the years, have helped refine my journalism. Thanks also to Jennifer Cockrall-King, Julie Van Rosendaal, Mary Bailey, Karen Anderson, Cindy Lazarenko, and Liane Faulder for inspiring conversations and lessons on food and writing about it.

Writing a book happens in the middle of real life, and it's here that I'd like to thank my extended family and friends—in particular Leah, Marshall, Kim, Sourena, Kasra, Sina, Frances, the Andruchow siblings and aunties, Sonja Kandera, Nola Keeler, Samara Jones, and Prasanna Bukka—who all have enriched my life with their love and wisdom. —TF

As an expat living away from Edmonton, I found this book a bittersweet endeavour. I miss my hometown and was reminded of that each time I dove into this work.

I have left lifelong friends whom I will never replace, but working on this book was an opportunity to remember, to celebrate, and to actively contribute to the place that made me who I am.

Special thanks goes to my husband, Dan. You help me see the bigger picture, and I know I can always count on you. Thanks for putting up with my nonsense.

Thank you to Mum, Dad, Emily, Hannah, and Papa for your unconditional love and support. I am always thinking of you and wishing we could share a meal together.

Thank you to my incredible friends who will always keep me missing Edmonton as long as I'm away. When I'm back with you, it feels like I never left.

Thanks especially to Sarah, for always having a moment to talk, for always opening up your home to me, and for being my bestie.

And to Dan N. for always making me laugh and realize whatever I'm worrying about is nothing.

To all my dear friends in Edmonton, this is for you. —LB

Index

Page numbers in italics refer to photos.

LEANNE BROWN is a writer and avid home cook born and raised in Edmonton but currently living in New York City. She believes everyone deserves to eat good food every day and that cooking is the key. Most recently, she wrote the award-winning, bestselling *Good and Cheap,* a cookbook of appealing, beautiful food for very low incomes. She has been delighted by cooking and baking ever since she realized that they were the closest things we have to magic.

TINA FAIZ loves to ask questions and loves to eat. It's no wonder this award-winning journalist's insatiable curiosity (and appetite) helps her unearth stories about food as well as politics, design, art, and culture for newspapers and magazines across the country, including the *Edmonton Journal, Calgary Herald, National Post, Ottawa Citizen, Vancouver Sun,* and *Montreal Gazette,* among others, and in a regular food column for CBC Radio. She's *Western Living* magazine's former Edmonton Editor and regularly judges food competitions in the city. When she's not writing, she is co-owner and strategist at Big Pixel Creative, helping clients use digital communications for social good.

ACME MEAT MARKET ·
PRAHA · THE BOTHY ·
· CANTEEN · CIBO BIS
CORSO 32 · CULINA · D
DOVETAIL DELICATES
SHOP · FILISTIX MO
HARDWARE GRILL · IZ
CHOCOLATE COUTUR
LITTLE BRICK · LITTL
NINETEEN · NONGBU ·
· RED OX INN · REMEDY
SHANGHAI 456 · SOFRA
CUISINE · THE SUGARB
TZIN · UNDER THE HIG
· VIVO RISTORANTE ·